"It was my honor and privilege to be a student under the tutelage of Dr. William 'Bill' Pannell. As a courageous trailblazer and role model of racial reconciliation and evangelism, Dr. Pannell's legacy as a teacher, preacher, and author lives on. I am forever grateful for the lasting impact he has on my life. In *A Merciful Journey* his wisdom and warnings are invaluable contributions for all people in our society and culture. I highly recommend it!"

—BRENDA SALTER MCNEIL

Author of *Becoming Brave: Finding the Courage to Pursue Racial Justice Now*

"Jesus said his followers were to be the light of the world. In Bill Pannell's case that meant both being a steady light and being an occasional lightning bolt for the mercy and justice of God's kingdom. This was especially needful inside the white, evangelical circles in which he ministered for many decades. Why and how this came to be—the price and beauty of such courage and faithfulness—are contained in this unfinished memoir. His thoughtfulness and humor, his honesty and passion affected so many. He shocked me and changed me, and I could not be more grateful."

—MARK LABBERTON

President Emeritus, Fuller Theological Seminary

"The legacy and impact of the late Rev. Dr. William E. Pannell cannot be overstated. This memoir is the timely and necessary reflection of a brilliant mind and devoted disciple of Jesus. Bill forces all of us to take a close look at what we believe the Gospel calls us to, and whether or not we've committed ourselves to that very call. May we each be inspired, right now, to walk in love and mercy."

—DWIGHT A. RADCLIFF JR.

Academic Dean for the William E. Pannell Center for Black Church Studies, Fuller Theological Seminary

"All significant institutions have seminal leaders. The beloved Bill Pannell was one of those for Fuller Seminary. He was a seed planter who made a substantial difference to individuals and the institution during his service as a trustee then a faculty member. Snippets of his life and work conveyed in this memoir help to give more insight into how the Lord led Bill and can lead us into places we never dreamed to go."

—DAVID EMMANUEL GOATLEY

President, Fuller Theological Seminary

A Merciful Journey

Rev. Dr. William E. Pannell (1929–2024)
Professor Emeritus of Preaching
Fuller Theological Seminary

A Merciful Journey

The Memoir of Bill Pannell

WILLIAM PANNELL

Introduction by Anthea Butler

Afterword by Jemar Tisby

CASCADE *Books* • Eugene, Oregon

A MERCIFUL JOURNEY
The Memoir of Bill Pannell

Cascade Books
An Imprint of Wipf and Stock Publishers
199 W. 8th Ave., Suite 3
Eugene, OR 97401

www.wipfandstock.com

PAPERBACK ISBN: 979-8-3852-7787-2
HARDCOVER ISBN: 979-8-3852-7788-9
EBOOK ISBN: 979-8-3852-7789-6

Cataloguing-in-Publication data:

Names: Pannell, William, author. | Butler, Anthea, introduction. | Tisby, Jemar, afterword.

Title: A merciful journey : the memoir of Bill Pannell / William Pannell; Introduction by Anthea Butler; Afterword by Jemar Tisby.

Description: Eugene, OR: Cascade Books, 2026.

Identifiers: ISBN 979-8-3852-7787-2 (paperback) | ISBN 979-8-3852-7788-9 (hardcover) | ISBN 979-8-3852-7789-6 (ebook)

Subjects: LCSH: Pannell, William E., 1929–2024. | Race relations—Religious aspects—Christianity. | United States—Race relations.

Classification: E184.A1 P325 2026 (paperback) | E184.A1 (ebook)

VERSION NUMBER 050126

Oh! I have slipped the surly bonds of Earth
And danced the skies on laughter-silvered wings;
Sunward I've climbed, and joined the tumbling mirth
of sun-split clouds,—and done a hundred things
You have not dreamed of—wheeled and soared and swung
High in the sunlit silence. Hov'ring there,
I've chased the shouting wind along, and flung
My eager craft through footless halls of air . . .

Up, up the long, delirious, burning blue
I've topped the wind-swept heights with easy grace
Where never lark, or even eagle flew—
And, while with silent lifting mind I've trod
The high untrespassed sanctity of space,
Put out my hand, and touched the face of God.

—John Gillespie Magee Jr., "High Flight"

Contents

Foreword

Peter Pannell

A Merciful Journey is a beautiful account of how God's purpose was carried out in my dad's life. Readers will come to appreciate how Dad interacted with the world with Christ at the center. Through poverty, pain, and disappointment (and given world wars, blatant hatred, and an ever-changing political system that masked the racism and social strife that often came from white evangelical "brothers and sisters"), Dad's life of devotion to Jesus serves as a model still relevant today. In particular, he had a certain way of helping us understand our Christlike responsibilities for loving all our neighbors.

My dad was rarely "Bill Pannell" to us. Something that he himself took much pride in, I think. After all, being husband and Dad is quite enough. Mom and Dad were married on October 15, 1955. Phil was born on November 9, 1957. I was born on March 1, 1962. According to my brother, I was supposed to be "Susan," which often came up during childhood trash-talking sessions between us. On Saturdays, Dad would be waiting for Phil and me to wake up. We would sleep-stagger downstairs with muffled good mornings. Dad would be waiting for us with fresh donuts and the TV on minutes before our favorite cartoon, *Johnny Quest*, began. We knew not all kids had it like this.

I recall a few years later, we welcomed our first color television. Mom took us with her to run errands. That was rare, us going with Mom. Turns out, Dad just needed to watch a baseball game in color without us boys jumping all over him. And Mom knew he needed that.

The first big-screen movies we saw as a family were *Patton,* with George C. Scott; *2001: A Space Odyssey*; and *Le Mans,* with Steve McQueen. My brother loved these movies. Me, well, I was a bit traumatized, so Mom took me separately to see *101 Dalmatians*, which in later years my brother used as further evidence that I should have been named Susan. Dad loved these movies because he was current! And as most know, he loved cars.

Whether in the summer or winter, when it was time for dinner and my dad was home, we would hear *the whistle*. My dad would whistle like no other man in the world. And when he did, his boys would come a-runnin' (or biking) as fast as our legs could run or peddle us home. It was dinner time, and it was no joke. Like church starting on time, this was a Pannell thing. We knew: *Do not be late.*

Dinner was never interrupted. We had a phone in the kitchen, the dial kind, and it was beige. I remember only one time when it rang during dinner. The time that my mother's brother passed away. Other than that, most people in our lives were having dinner at the same time. Dinnertime was sacred. When Dad was home, he read aloud to us after we ate. At times it was the Bible. But for years, he would read C. S. Lewis's Narnia series to us. My dad would orate, not just read. He played out every character . . . his face . . . his intonation. I remember thinking that Aslan, Peter, and Lucy were actually sitting at our table.

I know that this is Dad's memoir, but it would be difficult not to speak of Mom—especially since she did not write her own. I recently started cleaning out some of Dad's old items. In one of the drawers I found love letters from Mom to Dad. When he would go on speaking engagements for over a week, Mom would write to him. In one such note, Mom wrote,

> Dear Bill,
>
> Such a dreamy Sunday. The boys are taking a nap, and it has been raining all day. Peter is much better and although I shall send him to school tomorrow, I would feel much better about it if the sun would shine. Thank you so much for two very nice boys. They both said YUCK when Philip read aloud this card.
>
> The newspaper has an article today about low rates available in Florida now. This is what they call their off-season. I shall miss you terribly these next two weeks. I do like having you around.
>
> I love you,
> Hazel

Printed on the front of the card were the words "To my hubby on our anniversary. I love you for what you are!" On the inside: "MINE!" And in Mom's handwriting: "All 14 years!"

Dad loved my mom. Dad loved my brother and me. Dad loved his sisters and his brothers. But most of all, Dad loved his grandkids—Taylor, Grace, Eric, Ezekiel, and Justus. "Mercy!" he would declare, his voice a mix of astonishment and delight. The kids all called him "Pappa." Dad also had enormous love and respect for Luann—Phil's wife. After Phil died too young from prostate cancer, Lu would come over on Thursdays after a long day. They would have a glass of something along with Chinese food from a local eatery. Dad would give bits of advice, but mainly he would listen. Dad taught us all how to listen, and how to speak so that others would listen.

Dad also taught us how to throw and catch a baseball. How to play H-O-R-S-E in the backyard. How to tie a necktie, and how to properly hang up slacks with a sharp-edged crease. He taught us the importance of holding a door open for "a lady" and how to shake hands while looking into a person's eyes. He also taught us to love music. Dad loved Oscar Peterson, Ella, and William James "Count" Basie. Dad also loved hymns, and we loved listening to him sing them. He believed in their soulful connection with God.

But more than anything, Dad loved Jesus so much that he gave us to him. For him to protect us. To nurture us. To heal us. To discipline us. To save us. To love us. Or did Jesus give Dad to us, knowing that we would love Jesus because Dad loved him? Dad never pushed God—but his love for God was contagious. Dad was never in a room that Christ didn't occupy (especially whenever Michigan was playing Ohio State in football!).

This book's epigraph, "High Flight," is a poem that my brother and I heard our dad recite countless times during our childhood. The author, a young aviator-in-training, writes of the transcendent experience of flight, of climbing sunward and dancing in the skies "on laughter-silvered wings." What joy he must have known as he broke loose from "the surly bonds of Earth." In the end, the poet reaches out and touches the face of God. I wonder if Dad felt at home somewhere within these soaring words.

Recently, my son Ezekiel said, "I miss Pappa. I miss Pappa's words . . . what would he say to us?" First he'd ask, "How's your jump shot?" And then he would sing "Great Is Thy Faithfulness." He had a great voice. Dad would simply say, "Live with grace and keep loving one another."

As you read his memoir, we hope that you will come to love Dad and Mom just as we did.

Acknowledgments

Peter Pannell

Thanks to the many of you who came to our homes in Detroit and Altadena to talk with my dad. No matter the location, you laughed, prayed, and shared with Dad. Mom could often be found in the kitchen making the house smell loved. I know that these conversations were incredibly important to Dad, especially after Mom passed away. He valued you and relied on you all.

Thanks especially to Rob Johnston, for his many conversations with Dad, often over dinner that Rob's wife, Catherine Barsotti, had prepared. Rob promised Dad he would make sure that his memoir was published. He has shepherded this book to completion, including getting the contributions of Anthea Butler and Jemar Tisby, two of Dad's mentorees, whose words in these pages have beautifully captured the essence of his life's work. Their words and Dad's were copyedited with care by Arika VanDam and then shaped into final, published form by Rodney Clapp and the other good folks of Cascade Books. Together, you all have helped crystallize Dad's life and his importance for the white and black evangelical communities. Your love of Dad is evident in your significant contributions. Thank you.

Other friends and family of Dad deserve mentioning as well, for they helped him through their friendship and wisdom. To all who fought alongside Dad to address inequalities, isms, and what he would say was "just plain dumb behavior," thank you. These include Stanley Long, Richard Parker, Gerald Mann, Carl Ellis, Henry Greenidge, Ron Potter, John Perkins, and Ron White.

Finally, I would like to mention Mark Labberton and Joy Moore. As president of Fuller Theological Seminary, and as director of Fuller's Black Studies Institute, their leadership laid the foundation for Fuller's William E. Pannell Center for Black Church Studies—a center that is now working to empower black Christian leaders by focusing on cultural enrichment, racial reconciliation, and social justice. You can learn more about its important work at https://fuller.edu/pannell-center. Thank you, Mark, for your thoughtful care and intuition.

* * *

Editorial note: Our approach to Bill's writing was to let it remain his. His story to tell. His words. His voice. His life. Because his life included a time when people of color were referred to in terms that make some uncomfortable, we chose to leave those terms in their original form. They were part of his experience. Throughout the book, we confirmed details wherever possible and tried to fill in any missing or uncertain information (dates, names, places, etc.) by calling on family and friends and using any available resources. Occasionally there are content gaps that Bill clearly intended to come back to. We didn't try to fill those gaps but left them—including at the end, when he wraps up a chapter and then, to the reader's dismay, doesn't return to tell the rest of the story. His telling just stops; it's abrupt, and a letdown. Yet it's a testament to Bill's effervescent presence on the page and his abundant gifts as a storyteller that he leaves us wanting more, wishing he would or could have gone on for just a bit longer. We are grateful for what he gave us, though, and for having had the chance to help bring this writing of his into readers' hands and lives.

Introduction

Anthea Butler

Five months after the Los Angeles riots (or, as some call it, "uprising"), I met Bill Pannell at Fuller Seminary in Pasadena, California. It was the fall of 1992, and it was still a tense time in Los Angeles as the damage, recriminations, and rebuilding were being discussed and debated over the terrible outcome of acquittal of the policemen who beat Rodney King. As an African American woman starting a master's degree at a predominantly white evangelical seminary, I liked that all students of color met at orientation. What I remember most clearly about meeting Bill was what he said to all of us that day: "You need to learn how to milk this cow for all it's worth."

I was puzzled. I had been attending a Foursquare church, and no one had mentioned to me that I needed to know how to milk a cow! That was not the point. It was a deeper message, one rooted in the advantages and disadvantages of being African American and evangelical. The twoness of Bill's life meant that the culture of evangelicalism, racism, and his commitment to Christ would define his life and ministry.

The Rev. Dr. William "Bill" Pannell's life story straddles an important time of twentieth-century American history, evangelical history, and race relations. Born before the Depression and the division between fundamentalists and evangelicals, his life and witness for Christ was born in the crucible of race relations in America. These factors, along with his deep Christian faith, defined his ministry and life. The story you will read in these pages is not simply a memoir of his life but a chronicle of how both fundamentalism and evangelicalism shaped and defined an African

American man and his life. Bill Pannell, at his core, tried to point to the truth of the gospel while pointing to the sins of racism in America.

Bill's story helps to illuminate how race is often obscured by dominant narratives of evangelical endeavor. Bill's life, on one level, illuminates the experiences people often have when shifting from one framework of cultural experience to another. Bill's life was complicated and enriched by being a black man who challenged the narratives about American evangelicalism and race. He was one of the first to write about race and evangelicalism. In 1968 his book *My Friend, the Enemy* challenged the behavior and dominant narratives about evangelicals and their ways of dealing with race during the civil rights movement. He did it in such a way that he was both respected and revered for his truth-telling, despite the pressures to remain silent about race relations. For fundamentalists and evangelicals of color, the defining story about their faith is the way their contributions and faith were marginalized by the realities of racism in America.

It is important, then, to understand that this isn't simply Bill's autobiography. It is a history. A history of evangelicalism that incorporates the experiences of a black man who believed the message of the gospel, became a preacher and evangelist, yet had to contend with the original sin of America: racism. To fully understand Bill's life story, a bit of an introduction to the history that Bill lived in and through will help readers to understand not only his zeal for the gospel but, most importantly, his contributions to evangelicalism by confronting the racism embedded in the movement and in America.

Bill's life began in 1929, the year of the stock market crash that would be the start of the Great Depression. It was also the year that J. Gresham Machen resigned from Princeton Seminary. That event would not mean much to outsiders, but it was the beginning of a split that would define fundamentalism firmly and open the door to neo-evangelicalism in the 1940s and beyond. It also would shape Christian higher education. Fundamentalist schools like Fort Wayne Bible College (no longer in existence), where Bill attended, were about molding students for Christ, evangelism, and service to their communities. These schools did not want to engage the world, but to eschew it. It may be a surprise, then, to read in the pages of Bill's story that when he attended Fort Wayne Bible College, he did not know about the formation of the National Association of Evangelicals in 1942, Youth for Christ in 1944, or Fuller Seminary in 1947. The landmark *Brown v. Board of Education* decision in 1954 had not yet been made. Instead, Bill entered an encapsulated fundamentalism—keeping the world at bay while steeping congregations and students in the Bible. Even though fundamentalism formed the foundation of Bill's Christian life and witness, it did not keep him from embracing evangelicalism.

Bill would later play his own role in the history of evangelicalism in the twentieth century. His memoir is a personal story of an evangelist and seminary professor's life, but it is much more than that. It is history. Historians know a great deal about twentieth-century evangelicalism, but not much has been written about how ethnic evangelicals navigated these spaces until the 1970s and beyond. Bill, as an African American man, navigated the predominantly white world of American evangelicalism in the crucial organizational period from the 1940s to the 1980s. The massive social and political changes Bill lived through would define much of his writing, preaching, and teaching. His life also intersected with many of the movers and shakers of the twentieth century, men such as Billy Graham (Youth for Christ), C. Stacey Woods (InterVarsity), Jim Wallis (Sojourners), and Tom Skinner, who would become one of the major African American figures in evangelicalism in the late 1960s and 1970s. Bill's importance to the story of evangelicalism, then, is not simply as a bystander but as a participant in how the history developed, and how it was challenged on social and political issues.

Bill's life and witness can be described as "double consciousness," a term coined by African American sociologist W. E. B. DuBois to describe the dilemma of "twoness," of being American and Negro, and the disconnect between the two identities. In other words, the disconnect of being American, yet being treated as less, because of racism and Jim Crow. In Bill's life, the twoness was also being evangelical and black. White evangelicals during the 1950s and 1960s focused on promoting the message of the gospel, without a specific focus on racism or racial justice. Bill illuminates this issue in his story by recounting how much he did not know, because of attending a fundamentalist college, about early moments in the civil rights movement and the subsequent tensions about race in evangelical ministry. What set him on a different path than many evangelicals of the time was meeting black evangelicals like Tom Skinner in the 1960s and preaching and attending crusades in major East Coast cities like Newark, New Jersey. Proximity to other black religious leaders and the nascent black theology movement led by James Cone set Bill on a parallel trajectory to learn more about not only race relations in America but the larger cultural world outside of the evangelical movement. For Bill, and others like Skinner, the disconnect was between evangelicalism and being black, a disconnect increasingly challenged by the quest for justice through the civil rights movement.

That disconnect would lead to his first book, *My Friend, the Enemy*, which was about race relations in the church. In the book, published in the crucial year of 1968, Bill challenged white Christians to pay attention to their prejudices about race. While many would not receive the book in the spirit that it was meant, it would come to define the work that Bill was committed to—not only spreading the gospel but also confronting, improving, and illuminating the racial issues that existed in the evangelical community. His writing was sharp, direct, and unsparing in its assessment of white evangelicals. Toward the end of the book, Bill says succinctly, "I have no trouble believing that you want me in your church to sing on Sunday. I have very little faith you want me in your living room for serious discussion."[1]

A review of the book in *Christianity Today* in August of 1968 summarized Bill's rhetoric: "A stinging and slashing attack on white complacency, hypocrisy, paternalism, and smugness, the book sharply attacks white evangelicals in particular for failing to practice what Jesus taught."[2]

At the time, that book could have cancelled Bill Pannell out of both teaching and preaching at most major evangelical seminaries. Not at Fuller Seminary. David Allan Hubbard, president of Fuller, would intervene. He asked Bill to join Fuller Seminary as the first African American board member and later, in 1974, to join the faculty as assistant professor of evangelism and director of the Black Pastors' Program. This would eventually become the African American Church Studies Program, and now the William E. Pannell Center for Black Church Studies. At Fuller, he trained a generation of evangelical students, influencing black evangelical students intellectually and spiritually.

The year 1992 would be pivotal for Bill, not only because of being promoted to professor of preaching and dean of the chapel, but because of the April 29 outbreak of the Los Angeles riots. The city would burn over five days in the wake of the acquittals of the policemen who had mercilessly beat Rodney King. While there were "reconciliation" services and a religious gathering called Love LA, the racial tensions in Los Angeles persisted. Out of this came Bill's second book, *The Coming Race Wars? A*

1. William E. Pannell, *My Friend, the Enemy* (Waco, TX: Word, 1968), 123.
2. Dirk W. Jellema, "Evangelicals' Racial Paralysis," *Christianity Today* 12 (1968), 29.

Cry for Reconciliation, published in 1993. That book would become notable for evangelicals during the 1990s, frankly addressing the issues of race and class, evangelicals and the urban crisis, and his hopes for a revived Protestantism that would address the social ills of the times. One segment of the introduction stands out to me so clearly, and is prescient: "I fear we may be headed into an America with little time to read. We are on the very brink of a police state wherein law and order will mean something far more aggressive than it did when Richard Nixon inhabited the White House."[3]

I find myself thinking about what Bill would have to say about evangelicals and the state of our nation right now. He, as always, saw the racial issues clearly, yet wanted reconciliation and change. With the hardening of evangelicals who support tough immigration laws, the kind of reconciliation that he always called for seems to be distant and difficult in this fraught time. It does not mean, however, that the work he did was in vain. Far from it.

In telling his story, Bill is speaking about not simply his life experiences but what his hopes are for a better world. Bill recognizes the power of the gospel to change lives. But he wants to point toward the damage that racism does to people. For those of us who had the blessing to enjoy his wit, intellect, and witness, it is a great loss that he is gone. What a life he lived, and lived well. May these pages inspire you to work for changed hearts and minds.

3. William Pannell, *The Coming Race Wars? A Cry for Reconciliation* (Grand Rapids: Zondervan, 1993), 21.

Prologue

When interviewed about why it had taken ten years to finish his memoir, Gay Talese confessed: "It took me that long to figure out how to organize it." I read this with great relief since that has been my dilemma as I've attempted to write my own story. Where to start, what to include, what to leave out, and who would be interested in the thing.

The other insight that both informs and sobers me comes from Pico Iyer, a local writer who, in paying homage to a memoirist, observed that "the central question of any memoir, of course, is how much its writer comes to an understanding with the past; how well, that is, he gets on with forgiveness."

It has never been my ambition to write anything of book length about forgiveness, but if Iyer is even close to being right, then one would have no choice. After all, one is not born a writer, but one is born into a family, and into a society with all the complexities associated with that.

If one is also a Christian, particularly that "special" breed called "evangelical," ah, the necessity to consider the topic is well-nigh impossible to ignore. All that would be true if one were part of the majority culture in America. If one came from an African American family/community, the issue of forgiveness would be at the core of one's attempt to resolve the build-up of inner conflict over the years. The issue, of course, is identity.

It is this question of identity, with its peculiar twists in these United States, that shapes this work. I am still attracted to the insight of Stanley Crouch, who asserts that "within the context of our society, the 'I' and 'Thou' issue begets a very complex set of questions that cross the lines of class, of sex, of religion, of region, of color—which is what such questions should do." The celebrated literary critic, himself an African American, then makes a telling observation about fiction: "the most significant movement in American fiction is the turning away from the mono-ethnic novel in favor of the frontier where all the issues of integration are raised. From boy meets girl, to God and man, to goods and services, to low-down and dirty politics, integration is the most important theme in literature. That is all writers have ever talked about: how two things quite different or seemingly different can be brought together."

I suspect that this is true of any memoir. It has certainly been true of my life. It still is. So I expect that this will be a memoir of sorts, part memoir and part confession. The mood of the piece may be expressed in a statement by a character in James Sallis's novel *Cripple Creek*: "I had the overwhelming sense that my life was a book I'd only skimmed, one that deserved, for all its apparent insignificance, actually to be read." I have come reluctantly to the same conclusion.

PART 1

Formation: 1929–1951

1

An Unspoken Struggle for Identity

My pursuit of belonging may have begun when a white woman greeted my mother around the corner from our home in Sturgis, Michigan. I was being pushed in a buggy, and the white boy stood next to his mother. The women exchanged greetings—two women, one black, the other white.

They could not have known it, but their two boys, Morlan and William, would become lifelong friends. Morlan was the oldest by eight months. Beginning in kindergarten, they would attend the same schools, all the way through high school. Morlan played drums in the band, while William led the team from the locker room to the basketball court.

Mort would one day call upon his friend to officiate at his mother's funeral service. Years later, Mort's son Mike would request that William perform the ceremony at his father's funeral. Till death do us part. Lifelong friends, one black, the other white, in a small town in lower Michigan.

The city of Sturgis derived its name from one of its earliest founders. John Sturgis had settled on Sturgis Prairie in 1827 and became an enterprising farmer. He later became a judge. The town was named after him.

The Sturgis Prairie had already witnessed the struggle of native Americans who preceded white people there. Tecumseh had been there, as had the Potawatomi, the Chippewa, and the Ottawa. As the story goes, they sold their properties to white settlers or were driven off their lands by white militia sanctioned by government legislators.

A later struggle would involve early black settlers whose families established homes around a lake. Historians do not know what these early settlers called the lake, but white folks later called it "Nigger Lake." Located just east of the city limits, the place was shrouded in mystery. In all my years as a resident of Sturgis, I never knew of its existence. I never once heard mention of the lake or of these people. Could they have been early refugees from the travail of the American South?

The town of Sturgis was located equidistant between Detroit to the east and Chicago to the west. The major artery connecting these two cities was US 112, and it became our main street east and west. We called it Chicago Road. The town was also bisected by two railroad lines that linked parts of the state east-west and north-south.

I was born in 1929 at the Sturgis Memorial Hospital, just thirty-three years after Sturgis was incorporated. Without knowing it, I would be growing up with the town.

The hospital staff took one look at Mrs. Pannell's new son and decided to list his ethnicity as black. They could have chosen white or mulatto. But even then, the issue had nothing to do with color-spectrum absolutes. My friend Mort was Caucasian, but he wasn't white. None of my other friends were either. Unraveling this would become the unspoken soft underbelly of our struggle for a place in southern Michigan society.

I grew up in a pretty town with lovely tree-lined streets, paved sidewalks great for roller skating, and a main street lined with shops doing steady business. The house in which we lived was large, with a front porch complete with a swing. At the front of the house and along the north side was latticework covered with vines of some sort. This made for a very pleasant setting, a lovely vantage from which to view the street.

As for belonging, Sturgis had its social stratification network, and we all knew who the "swells" were. We caddied for them at the country club. Racism in Sturgis was of the gentlemanly sort; all men are created equal, some more than others. Growing up in Sturgis was idyllic. Almost. I have yet to get my hair cut in my hometown. The city was quietly bustling in both style and energy; its history was one of progress.

This town in lower Michigan was not very sophisticated about racial matters. It didn't need to be. A list of the names in the town's elite registry in the thirties and forties would reveal that the city had been settled by Europeans, and I came to know their names if not their faces. They were the early developers of the town's economic fortunes. I would later attend school with their offspring.

The city was possessed of great civic pride. Blessed with visionary and generous leaders, it boasted fine schools, a civic center, a town orchestra, and first-class facilities for semi-professional baseball and football teams. It was not uncommon for teams from Sturgis to compete against visiting professional teams from the fledgling professional football league. To support this growing civic development, the town fostered a climate that lured ambitious businessmen to its environs, giving rise to large manufacturing plants that made furniture and appliances, factories full of busy people churning out a living for the kids I went to school with.

They were all white. I knew of no black men or women who worked in those plants or in their offices. My hometown was run by white men; all the black men and women who worked outside their homes pushed mops, literally and symbolically.

One exception was William Jones, a black man who opened the Oaklawn Terrace Aquarium in 1934. He featured an array of goldfish, fifty-eight varieties of tropical fish, and various aquarium supplies. Four years later, Mr. Jones added thirty more tanks to his collection, bringing the total capacity of his business to 103 tanks. By this time, the store on Magnolia Avenue featured 105 varieties of tropical fish, an alligator, and two pet bullfrogs.

Mr. Jones was apparently also involved with the Sturgis Wildcats, a semi-pro football team. In a 1929 group picture of the team, Jones, referred to as "Willie" Jones, is listed as manager.

Another exception was Jack Mason, a black lineman for the Wildcats during the 1933 season. I recall him as an occasional visitor to our home, and he was enough a part of our family tree that we called him Uncle Jack.

2

The Heart of the Home

William Davison and his wife, Anna, were pioneers of African American life in Sturgis. Anna was a talented seamstress. Pictures of her, together with her two young daughters, testify to her stylish imagination.

Her daughters, Edna and Olive (my mother), took an active part in black social life as it ranged from Sturgis west to Three Rivers and Vandalia. Edna was the older of the two girls and possessed a lovely voice. Her early ambition was to become a nurse. She had the temperament for it. Olive was a talented pianist. She was active in high school and responsible for providing the music that signaled the changing of classes. A favorite picture of mine is of her seated in front of a four-man jazz group or group of musicians. She was the pianist.

Olive went on to study music at the Chicago Conservatory. It was there that she met and married John Bromfield. The marriage was short-lived, due in large part to the opposition of Mr. Bromfield's parents.

Dispirited and deeply disappointed, the young musician met William Pannell, and a budding romance ensued, culminating in marriage. They named their first child, a son, William Edward. The couple settled in Sturgis, living with Olive's parents. A year and a half later, the couple welcomed a daughter, naming her Beverly Joan.

William and Olive's early years of marriage and family life were difficult. The country was deep into the Depression. In 1935, six years after their son's birth, fully one-eighth of the town's population of seven thousand were on some form of relief. Finding a job in town was nearly impossible for most white men, let alone a man of color.

William Pannell was very light complexioned and probably could have passed for someone other than African American. His mother might have been from Mexico, or a small village in Spain. His father was from the big city of Chicago. He finally gave up on job hunting in Sturgis and began work as a cook on passenger trains that sliced their way through the territories between Detroit and Chicago and westward to Los Angeles. Along the way he became an accomplished cook, and years later we would argue over the necessity of wine at a festive table. He could not tolerate the idea that his son was studying for the ministry possessed with such archaic notions that Jesus drank grape juice. Later I could admit that he was right.

But Dad's absence from the family became an issue between the couple, and they separated. Dad returned to Chicago, and Mom stayed in Sturgis with her two children.

Grandpa William Davison didn't run anything in the town. He was the night watchman at the Berridge Shear Company. Grandpa had shown me his workplace, and I was so proud to be with him in the grown-up world. I can still smell the oil-soaked shavings on the shop floor. The factory lay adjacent to the railroad tracks that divided the town east and west.

The best part of Grandpa's work, as far as we were concerned, was his return to the house in the early mornings. His clothes would smell of the factory, and he would wash before proceeding into the day. To Beverly and me, his coming meant that we would likely have breakfast with him. The ritual was always the same: first, he had to make a fire in the pot-belly stove, then go across the street to Mr. Reich's grocery store, where he would purchase rolls or donuts. By the time he returned, Sis and I would be perched at the top of the stairs, staring intently at the floor below and in chorus asking if the fire was ready. "Is the fire ready, Grandpa?" When he assured us that all was ready, we would bound down the stairs and proudly have breakfast with Grandpa: milk laced with a bit of coffee, and donuts. Heavenly. I always thought it was nice that Grandpa could live with us, in our house. In fact, we were living in his house.

I do not know how my mother met Joe Perkins. My first recollection of Mr. Perkins came on a visit to Howe Military Academy. The academy was located several miles south of the city limits and anchored the town of Howe, Indiana. Like most academies, the place served as a haven for the sons of the well-off. The school became a terminus for young black men from mid-south Kentucky.

I don't recall that Dad Perkins spent much time reading, whether the *Daily Journal* or a book, and that was probably due to his lack of formal education. Crab Orchard, Kentucky, didn't expend much effort in educating young black boys. His favorite music was a mix of country and blues, both expressions strange to the ears of kids raised in Michigan. His talk of Joe Louis's defeat at the hands of Max Schmeling in their historic 1936 bout was my first awareness of racial solidarity, but it would take years before I caught up with its significance.

The man had few vices. He drank some whiskey; there was usually beer in the house. I liked the taste of beer, especially when Mom would let us put salt in it and watch it bubble into a nice foam. Dad Perkins rarely got drunk, but when he did, I found it embarrassing and disgusting. Drinking did not make him violent or even loud. Just silly.

His real vice was smoking, although in those days no one would have called it a vice. It was a habit that upset me because I thought it was a waste of needed money for the family. Milk was more important than tobacco. Years later we would wonder if his smoking had contributed to the ill health of Mom—secondhand smoke.

Joe Perkins fathered six children with my mother: four girls and two boys. Edna, Olive, David, Sarah, Richard, and Maryanne. Including Beverly and me, ours was a household of eight children. I was the oldest.

Mom was the heart of our home. My strongest images of her were those associated with the piano and the rocking chair. She sat with such ease at the piano, and music flowed effortlessly from her fingers. She seemed to be at peace while playing, a joyful contentment about her.

Then there were the babies. As a kid I watched with fascination as she brought another baby home from somewhere. The hospital, I guessed. I knew nothing about pregnancy or how that mystery happened, so I observed nothing about her appearance before she disappeared from the house. The babies seemed to belong wherever they came from, and they were dearly loved. Mom breastfed them all, as I'm sure she had me, and it was clear that the intimacy associated with that ritual was a source of pleasure for her. It was also a source of fun for me as I delighted in causing just enough of a ruckus to make the baby fuss. Mom's scolding for this was mixed with humor.

My mother was the disciplinarian in the house. She had her little switch, and she wielded it with precision on our rear ends and legs. But she never exhibited anger or bitterness in this. She was the voice of discipline, the solid presence who gave us direction in our behavior toward each other. She was fair in her directions to Beverly and me, although I often thought she didn't pay enough attention to the needs of a boy to get away from his sisters.

This became especially painful when Beverly got her bicycle. Uncle Shelton had bought me a bike some time before, and it set me free to roam the neighborhood and even other parts of the city. My friends and I raced each other and felt we were the kings of the road.

Then came a bike for Beverly, and she wanted to keep up with me. I was not pleased with that arrangement, but Mom didn't seem to realize what a drag she became. She would cry, and Mom would relent, and I was instructed to let her ride along, at least sometimes.

Beverly contracted tuberculosis in her late teens. She struggled with the disease as it settled in her bones. Upon her release from a hospital in Ann Arbor, she chose marriage. I wasn't happy with her choice and I'm sure I sounded like the older brother as I let her know how I felt. I asked her if the guy was a Christian. She replied that he was a member of a church. Unsatisfied, I pressed her more. She responded by telling me to bug off.

The couple moved to Three Rivers, a small town twenty miles or so from our hometown. We played them in sports and the rivalry was intense. Compared to Sturgis, Three Rivers was Hicksville. My sister's marriage produced three children, but they struggled with growing up in a town not known for its hospitality toward people of color. Or toward anyone trapped in the low end of the town's economics and culture.

The town of Sturgis was hit hard by the Depression. During the early 1930s, many people were struggling to get by. Yet the town rallied behind its civic-minded leaders in industry and commerce. We kids drank milk from cartons and ate graham crackers supplied by local merchants. Churches and the American Legion, along with other welfare agencies, pitched in to relieve townspeople trapped in joblessness. Even the local theater helped; it gave free tickets to its movies, with apples and bananas for kids. A local tobacco company offered free cigars to the menfolk.

By 1941, when I was twelve years old, we could have bought a six-passenger Packard sedan for $990 dollars or a Cadillac for $1,345. Gasoline for these expensive cars was 17.9 cents a gallon for premium. An eight-room house could be bought for $4,500. More to our concerns was coffee at 30 cents a pound, and a pound of Constantine butter for 38 cents. Two packages of Wheaties could be had for 19 cents, and a dozen fresh eggs sold for 17 cents. One could get out of town, from Sturgis to Detroit and back via Greyhound Bus Lines, for $3.40 round trip.

3

A First Exposure to Politics

We had no idea what was going on in the world beyond the house and school. Neither politics nor culture was discussed at our house, at least not within earshot of the kids. Of course, both were topics of talk among the adults. Whenever black people gathered, they found it necessary to talk about white folks and the world they created for the rest of us.

My first exposure to politics came with the bombing of Pearl Harbor by the Japanese in 1941. I recall the drama of President Roosevelt's speech announcing that a state of war existed between our countries. Early radio broadcasts spoke of the carnage of the war, and it was splayed across the newsreels at the Strand Theater. We were at war, and that was as real to me as a Western starring Tom Mix.

War came to wear the familiar faces of Hollywood actors raising money for war bonds—actors like James Cagney and John Wayne, and many others, supporting those who bravely defended the nation against the pagans from Germany and Japan. Especially Japan. They were slant-eyed and colored, a menacing combination that even white Germans under Hitler could not match. And by the time the propaganda machines were turned loose on us, we gladly gave up friends, sons, and daughters to this effort.

My second exposure to the war came at baseball practice. We were at Spence Field throwing balls, hitting fungoes, when someone mentioned the death of President Roosevelt. One of the guys remarked that he got what he deserved. Good riddance, he said. He was promptly hit on the cheek by one of the other guys, and a fight broke out that amazed me. I knew then that politics meant more to those guys and their families than it did to us.

We had learned about Roosevelt because of his famous speech before Congress denouncing Japan's "sneaky" aggression at Pearl Harbor. I recall the drama that speech and the accompanying newsreels produced among the theatergoers. We were at war, and that came to mean stamps for all sorts of goods—food, gasoline, and so on. With the stamps also came visits from white people from across town, people who were acquainted with Mom but who didn't usually venture into our neighborhood. I have no idea what we received in exchange for our stamps. Good will, probably. What Joe Perkins really needed was a better job.

We were patriots, of course. Having been raised on the stories of pilgrims and Valley Forge and images of George Washington, supplemented by the likes of Tom Mix and the Lone Ranger, we knew that it was our destiny to withstand all our enemies, domestic or foreign, as the phrase goes. We collected everything from scrap iron to waste fats for the making of nitroglycerin and other explosives for the war effort. We bought war stamps; others bought bonds. We pooled our pennies at school for the stamps, and I contributed a bit of artwork by painting a replica of a P-51 on the wall fronting our high school study hall. We even attempted to raise money for the purchase of its real counterpart. When it came to war, we were really into it. And when Slim Werkhaven, a test pilot from Ypsilanti, buzzed our town in his B-24, we were all the more jazzed about our efforts. And glad that his daughter was one of the school's students.

Years earlier I had seen my first anti-war film, *The Dawn Patrol*. Howard Hawks had attempted to raise some questions about the efficacy of wars, given the toll they took on the young men who fought them. What, after all, was the point of it all? I didn't understand any of this, content with the anxiety of seeing my favorite actor play the leading role. Errol Flynn had ruled Sherwood Forest and had carved up evil old Basil Rathbone in one of the greatest sword fights in movie history. So of course he would prevail against the Germans in the skies over Europe. But he didn't; he was shot down by a German ace, and when his goggles were dropped at the feet of his comrades at their airstrip, I was thrown into confusion.

On the way home I asked Mom for some explanation of what I had just seen. Surely, he had not died. Maybe he would show up later, I reasoned. All I remember is her words, "Maybe so." But I was left with an emptiness I could not explain until I saw the film again many years later. It was the only film I recall ever seeing with my mother. The year was 1938. It was the first inkling that Europeans, and hence we Americans, were not invincible in war. It would take many years for this idea to really become reality, in a place called Vietnam.

4

The Lone Ranger and Tonto

My life was wrapped around my friend Mort Jellison. He and I spent hours together. I was at his house and he at mine, although I was at his more than ours, and I think that was because our house was full of girls.

Mort and I fished in nearby Minnewaukon Lake, occasionally from a boat loaned to us by a resident. Nothing like the tug of a bluegill on the end of a cane pole. Unless it was a feisty bass plunging the bobber into the depths trying to fling the lure from its mouth.

Minnie, as she was affectionately called, was a better lake for fishing than Crotch Lake north of town, even from the shore. For some reason Crotch Lake had an uppity air about it, a middle-class version of Klinger Lake where some of the town's would-be swells had summer homes and cottages. Minnie was closer too, and that helped when Mort and I pushed our hoops up Centerville Road, out past Kirsch Airport. It was two miles from Mort's house to the lake. Later, when we really advanced with our toys, we pushed large rubber tires over the same terrain.

I followed Mort everywhere, even though I knew that I was quicker and faster on foot than he. The chemistry between us was akin to that between brothers. I admired him greatly and envied his station in life. He was white. His dad made good money and owned a car. His sled was bigger than mine. He had trains to play with. While he was generous with his stuff, he also made it clear that it was his stuff.

When we walked home from the Saturday afternoon cowboy flicks, he insisted on being the hero of the movie. He was the Lone Ranger, of course, and I was Tonto; his horse was white, mine was spotted; his white horse was faster than my spotted one. He was Tom Mix or Hopalong Cassidy. He didn't know that he knew it, but already it was becoming clear to both of us that white was better than colored, be it black, brown, red, or yellow.

Movies were a big part of our lives. We preferred Westerns, and our favorite tactic on a Saturday was to time our arrival at the theater just before the prices changed for the night snows. We could get in for ten cents and still have a nickel for candy. In those days a nickel could get you a seriously big Baby Ruth bar that would last half the day if you ate it carefully. We would often stay for the midnight show, which actually started around ten o'clock.

One of our favorite sports was shooting birds. We made slingshots from tree branches, perfect V's connected by strips of rubber cut from inner tubes. We developed keen eyes, and no bird was safe, be it robins pilfering cherries in our backyard or starlings lined up on high wires bordering the factory up the street.

If I was a better shot with my sling shot, Mort's mother made better jams than mine did. After spending half a day making sure the world was safe from marauding Indians and crooked white men selling them booze and guns, we'd head for his mom's kitchen where she would make sandwiches of bread, butter, and strawberry jam. Or we would raid the bushel baskets brimming with apples his father kept in the garage. They were juicy and cool in the fall and winter.

Christmas was an event of mixed emotions, of high expectations tempered by the realities of scarcity. In our house the tree was ever present and properly decorated, heightening our anxieties. Our hope was that Santa would be generous, and quite specifically attuned to our wants; our fear was that the old geezer would be as forgetful that year as he had been in the past. Most of the stuff I wanted usually ended up at Mort's house.

I later found out that Santa was really Mr. Jellison's workplace, where toys were handed out to employees at Christmas.

I learned at Christmas that Mort's folks were better off than we were. The difference was that Mort's dad was white and had a better job than Joe Perkins.

But for two young boys that didn't seem to make any difference.

5

Biology Was a Bore

SCHOOL WAS FUN—FOR THE most part. The teachers were pleasant if undemanding. I had no ambitions to be a scholar, so my chief concern was making sure I was eligible for whatever sport was being played during the year.

I was a typical teenager trying to navigate the routines of school. I liked high school and did fairly well academically. Biology was a bore, but I liked history and literature. I wrote for the class paper and was inducted into Quill and Scroll, an international honor society of high school journalists. I was the secretary of our local chapter. I sang in the school's chorale, which performed at civic gatherings and in-school occasions.

I can think of only a couple of outstanding teachers, and just one who could inspire students to think, to explore an idea, to get to the core of an argument. High school was solid, foundational stuff, but it did little to push the boundaries of my world or extend the horizons of possibility. We were shaped by words in the service of insuring that we would become good citizens. The words were those expressive of the democratic experiment called "liberty and justice for all." Only it wasn't taught as an experiment. We were assured that whatever the founding fathers had in mind, it was very close to ultimate political truth. It might even have been sent down from heaven. We never questioned any of it; to do so would have meant that we had become unpatriotic. I can't recall any attempt by our history teachers to help us unpack the significance of the Civil War.

My lone exposure to literary culture came because of an invitation by William Smith, the school's English and speech teacher. He said he wanted me to try out for a part in the school's annual play. It was to be a rendition of Thornton Wilder's *Our Town*.

I was taken aback by his suggestion, never having heard of the play, nor ever having thought of myself as an actor. He thought he saw something in me, I guess, and I won the part of the stage manager. The play was an enormous success and played to full houses for three nights instead of the usual one-night stands. Mr. Smith said I should become an actor. That experience served to stimulate something deep inside, and I knew, beyond knowing, that there was more to my future than basketball.

One day I was seated in biology class listening to Mr. DeWitt try to elicit some response from his sleepy group. The fire horn that went off mid-class was a welcome break from my slumber. Since the fire station was only a half block from school, when the horn sounded, we knew there was a fire somewhere in town. The engines roared past our window. The sounds disappeared in the distance. Back to the boredom.

At noon I headed home for lunch and was met on the way by Mrs. West. She had been waiting beside her car, and she approached to tell me the bad news. It was our house that had caught fire that morning. She offered me a ride home, and there it was—the place had been severely burned throughout the downstairs, and the rest of the house was damaged by smoke. It seemed that someone had forgotten to pull the plug on the iron as they dashed for school. It was a good thing I went to school that morning. I had decided to skip and sleep in before. I could do that and still make it to baseball practice in the afternoon. But somehow my conscience awakened even if my body didn't, and I jumped out of bed, dressed, and ran to catch my 8:30 class. I failed to notice the ironing board.

Mom said fire was the one thing she had always feared. She worried about her kids of course, but she need not have fretted too deeply. We were the concern of neighbors and friends. Beverly, Edna, and Olive were taken in by Henry and Leona Bunch. Dickie and Sarah went with Aunt Edna, and Mrs. West and her husband, Herbert, opened their home to me. Dad Perkins decided to shovel out a place on the location and stayed in the house. David stayed with him.

Our family was not immune from that "awful" notification that relatives from the South were interested in coming North. Many families like ours had been in touch with relatives in the South but had not expected that one day they might decide to settle up North. They would come North without a place to stay while they got settled, found work, and enrolled their children in school. Meanwhile, they would expect a welcome from their dear relatives.

My stepfather's brother wanted to relocate to Sturgis and needed a place to stay until he could get settled. He would bring his wife and children with him. So imagine a houseful of two husbands, two wives, and nine kids. Whining, runny-nosed kids who were always hungry for "yite bread." I never did like them. The house was too small for them and us, and I had no experience, no understanding, of what was going on in the lives of black people in the South.

Gussie was a nice man, quiet, as was his wife. They stayed with us for more than two years and finally found a house on the south end of town. We felt liberated. The refrigerator was ours again, and so was all the milk therein. All the beds were occupied but with us kids.

School might have been different had I been enrolled in a pre-college curriculum. My grades did not allow for such, or perhaps someone decided my prospects beyond athletics were not promising enough for a post-college career. Whatever the circumstances, I was not really interested in ideas. Math was pure drudgery, except for algebra. I did have a liking for literature and history, but subject matter didn't seem to be leading anywhere except a grade and eligibility on Friday nights. Truth be told, I had no ambitions for college. Without realizing it, by the time I had become an eleventh grader, I was lost; college was one of the last places I aimed for.

While in school I felt I was growing up in a society that did not have a place for me. I was not invited to join the clubs in school that seemed to be stepping stones to life after school, such as the Commercial Club. They were clubs that could connect one to business or careers that mattered.

My classmates had begun pairing off, socializing and setting themselves up for the big occasions of prom and post-game dances at the American Legion Post. They had their Friday evening gatherings, square dancing at my friend Jack Grim's place. I did get invited to that one once, but I had trouble feeling at ease. I never learned to dance, no matter what kind of dance.

6

Anything That Bounced

My early interests focused on sports. Anything that bounced. We played football in the side yard, I and my friends. My sister Edna liked to play too, and she was good. She was joined by a neighbor girl, Phillis Mast, and we included them because they were good. Edna was the only sister who could play, and sports became her lifelong diversion.

The yard beside our house ran the length of the property, until it merged with the garden. A large cherry tree and an apple tree separated the yard from the garden, and they also served as the boundary for our touch football games. By early fall, the grass was well worn from these skirmishes. We had no money for footballs, so we stuffed sugar sacks with leaves.

My school classmates played with me. I especially liked playing with Bill Krontz, even though he wasn't very athletic. Later, Cleon Nodestein became my competition. By then we had real footballs. In high school, Cleon was a star player, while I was relegated to manager. But I was also the one who did the kicking on fourth down, just like we had played it when we were kids.

I discovered I could find success in sports. I came to imbibe the town's pride in athletic achievement. Sports was my way out, my way of escape from the boredom of academic life. I lettered in football. I would have played on a golf team if we had had one.

By early high school, Dean Sidener and I spent hours playing catch with whatever baseball we could find. He always had more pop on his fastball and a better curve, and it became clear to me that if I played baseball in high school, it wouldn't be as a pitcher. I played shortstop.

Our basketball team won the state championship when I was a sophomore. I was able to secure a ride to East Lansing, the location of Michigan State University, my first exposure to a major college setting. When I returned to school, I wrote about the event as the sports editor of the school paper.

My love of sports, especially basketball, seemed to be an all-American occupation. It didn't serve as a way out of a ghetto lifestyle, as it was for many black young people. I simply loved the game and played it well.

I was a member of the Varsity Club, composed of all the guys who lettered in sports. I lettered in three: basketball, football, and baseball. I capped off my senior year in sports by being nominated to the first team, all-Twin Valley basketball team. Years later I was inducted into the Bible College Hall of Fame.

Because of sports I became a presence on campus.

7

Learning About Jesus

I WAS A JUNIOR in high school when I was invited to attend a Halloween party at a church. The pastor's daughter, who was in my grade, had invited me. Eunice and I were attracted to each other. She played in the band, and I called her Speed as she seemed to be in motion most of the time.

The party was held in the parsonage and featured games and plenty of food. I knew some of the kids there, as they too were in the same grade. Some I had known since kindergarten. Most of the kids in our class went to church somewhere.

The earliest church in Sturgis was Methodist, followed by the usual denominations—Baptists, Roman Catholics, and of course Episcopalians.

If Mrs. Pannell would later be put off by the racism of a member of the Presbyterian Church, Mrs. Jellison and her family would be offended by the classism of the Methodists. Seems that when they showed up for Sunday worship, they didn't look the part, their clothes bearing testimony to the fact that most of the city was working class, hardly able to survive the Depression years. They were turned aside at the front door—or, more likely, asked not to return until they could dress properly for Sunday morning. Racism and classism were deeply ingrained in the town from its inception. The family never went back.

Depending on the social status of their parents, kids my age were either Baptists, Methodists, or Presbyterians. Toss in a couple of Nazarenes, and you had the spread.

I was from none of these churches. Our family's exposure to church life was nil. Mom confided in me that she had been attracted to the Presbyterian Church but had been turned away by a racist remark from a member. She never went back, and when it came time to decide what church to send her kids to, she chose none of them. Her favorite reading seemed to be a devotional from the Christian Science Church. She seemed to derive comfort from this reading, if not salvation. She never talked with us about salvation or being saved. Mom taught us to pray, as we went to bed each night, "if I should die before I wake."

Mom's aversion to church changed when Otto Meade and his wife asked if she would allow Beverly and me to attend Sunday school. They were members at the Gospel Hall. I doubt that Mom knew much about the teaching of the hall, but she did know the Meades, and she trusted them. The couple were part of the neighborhood. Otto's mother lived next door to us. They cared about us, and from our first exposure until high school, we attended that church. We never did know what they believed beyond what they taught us. This was due in large part to the fact that we were not invited to attend church where the adults attended. And the adults met to sing hymns, listen to a sermon, and take communion: what they called the Lord's Supper. They did this routine every Sunday. They were an offshoot of First Baptist, part of the Brethren Assemblies of America (Plymouth Brethren). We learned about Jesus in Sunday school class and from the "pieces" we committed to memory and recited at sacred events such as Easter and Christmas. We sang choruses, the most prominent of which was the one celebrating Jesus and his love. "Jesus loves me, this I know, for the Bible tells me so." Ah, the Bible.

But the Meades were not the only ones at the church who expressed concern for us. As the congregation grew, they bought a small bus and did everything but get us out of bed to ensure our presence at Sunday school. As our family grew, the younger ones became part of this Sunday morning ritual too. A lovely picture of the young people of that Assembly shows all our siblings in attendance.

The person most responsible for my sensitivity to spiritual matters was Shirley Griffith. He was a businessman whose jewelry store was next door to the town's pool hall. By the time I got to high school, I had outgrown Sunday school. I had moved on to more important pursuits such as sports and pool. Along with friends from school and the team, we would meet after practice and shoot pool on our way home. In addition to that splendid pastime, the place also had the best chocolate sundaes in town. We would shoot pool, load up on a sundae if we had the money, and go home for supper. I didn't always have money for all of that.

Then there was Mr. Griffith. He could be seen standing outside his door watching us kids move in and out of the poolroom. He would smile at me and greet me with such warmth and good will. And he assured me that I was missed at Sunday school. He did not preach or scold. No frowns. Just that smile and warmth. Had I words at the time, I would have known that I could have walked straight into his open arms. He stood by the door.

Years later, many years, it seems, I would stop by his store and announce that I had found the woman I wanted to marry. He was pleased, welcomed me into the place and proceeded to give me the rings that would grace her lovely third finger, left hand. I had finished Bible college, had entered the ministry and joined a congregation in Detroit associated with the Christian Assemblies, Plymouth Brethren.

It was this background and sensitivity that I brought to the Missionary Church when Eunice Randall, the pastor's daughter, invited me to the Halloween party. Eunice and I teased each other in study hall, and I was glad to attend so that I could see her. I was surprised at how much fun we had. I didn't know Christian young people could have so much fun. There was plenty to eat, and we played games and laughed our way through the evening. I was hooked. I had no intention to join the church or "get saved." I did intend to get saved before I died, of course. Later. No one in his right mind intended to go to hell, I thought. But it was within this group of young people that I did profess Christ. I went forward in the annual revival meeting there, and with conviction dripping off my nose, I knelt at the altar and gave my heart to Jesus. It was April of 1946.

My conversion was good news to the family. But I was not the first member of the clan to profess faith. Edna had become a Christian through the ministry of the First Baptist Church. Mom seemed pleased with our interest in religion, pleased that we had become Christians, but expressed no interest in following in our steps.

I suspect that the one person who may have kept Mom's spiritual interests in mind was Mrs. Bunch. She was in and out of our home, not on a regular basis, but when she came, she brought a spirit of godliness with her. And Mom needed an older woman to steady her during some difficult years while raising her growing family.

But it wasn't just her family she had to raise. Our home had become a hostel for visiting musicians who couldn't find a place to stay while performing at local clubs. These were temporary jobs, but we got stuck with these people, mostly men. They probably made some contribution to the family coffers while staying with us, and several of them were fun to be with. Mom was careful to see to it that they weren't too friendly with my sisters. Our house became a temporary home for the relatives of black friends who had been in the town for a while but who had no permanent residences.

8

An Uncommon Path Forward

We had no inkling that our mother was ill. I can't recall her coughing or struggling to walk or being absent from our usual routines as a family. She had gone to the hospital but had stayed only one day. She returned home. Auntie said that she had a miscarriage.

Then, two or three days later, I sat with her on the front porch, at a loss for words. I knew she was leaving for the hospital, but I had no words. Finally, I told her it was time for me to get back to school. She said, "Do you have to go so soon?" I answered in the affirmative, and we said goodbye. I still see the sadness in her eyes. She was gone when I returned from school that day. She never returned. It was the loneliest day of my life.

The sanitarium in Battle Creek had been founded by Seventh-day Adventists as an expression of their faith and commitment to a holistic lifestyle. The emphasis throughout its history, beginning in 1866, was on health care and recovery based on the observance of nature's provisions—sunshine, exercise, lots of fresh water, and a healthy overall diet, with a heavy emphasis on nuts.

I did graduate from high school. Mr. Bunch saw to it that I was properly attired for the occasion. He had driven me to South Bend, Indiana, where a new suit was purchased—deep brown, double-breasted, with a dark pinstripe for a sophisticated accent.

Other graduates received wristwatches. Had I a choice, I would have chosen one, but that luxury would have to wait a few years. Besides, my thoughts were on the immediate future and what it might hold for me, where I was headed, and with whom I would travel.

The future was clouded by the sickness of my stepfather. I can't recall the malady, but it was sufficient to threaten our family's well-being. Joe Perkins was our only source of income.

When he came to me to suggest that I ought to assume that role, and that I could probably secure work at Freeman, where he labored, I was agitated. Scared really.

In the first place, I had an aversion to work. At least to that kind of work: factory work, sweeping a floor, cleaning up the dusty shop floor, full of lint and manufacturing debris.

We learned years later that it was this dusty atmosphere that contributed, along with his chain smoking, to the onset of emphysema, which would ultimately claim Joe's life.

Apart from this aversion, I also had a fear that to begin working in a factory would mean never leaving. All the black men in town pushed mops or worked in private family situations. They labored with quiet resolve and dignity, raised their families, sent their children to school. White fathers did the same things, of course, and they were hard-working factory people. Nothing wrong with that. But I was wary of this. I also knew of classmates whose life trajectory was not factory work, and I knew that they were really not much smarter than I was. Better connected maybe, but not smarter. And they were headed for colleges. They seemed to know what the future held or what they wanted out of life. I had no such assurances.

These questions were finally settled by a woman named Mildred, who would suggest an uncommon path forward for my young life.

Mildred Bedford was a domestic in the household of one of the city's wealthy businessmen. Charles Spence was already a legend in the city. He was the leading philanthropist. His name was stamped on key enterprises in the city, ranging from the country club to the stadium where semi-pro football was played, and where we would play our high school games of football and baseball. His name was also displayed at the town's airfield north of the city. He was also president of one of the town's banks.

Mildred worked for him, as did Henry and Leona Bunch. Henry and Leona were formative figures in the life of our family, especially Beverly and me. An early and much-treasured black and white photo has Leona holding a months-old baby while seated on the front steps of a stately looking house. I was that baby.

Leona was the best cook I have ever met. Henry was a model of quiet sophistication. When he drove the family car for Spence, a lovely Cadillac, he was the picture of proper elegance and reserve.

One of my fondest memories of him was a trip to Indianapolis. He invited me to go with him, just the two of us. I was in the fourth grade. We spent several days in the Indiana capitol, at least in that part of it where black people lived. Mr. Bunch owned property there and had gone for business reasons. So his wife, Leona, would pray for his soul, and Henry would look after the business of keeping her solvent.

Mildred was largely invisible in that household. She was single, slight of build, light-complexioned, and seemingly content to remain in the background in the network of domestics in the city. Mrs. Bunch was Pentecostal, a Jesus-Only Pentecostal. Mr. Bunch was a Baptist whose single vice was an occasional cigar. Leona was critical of this habit, seeing in it another example of his lack of holiness. Her vice was a love of Coca-Cola.

Mildred was content to align herself with the local chapter of the Salvation Army. She seemed to delight in helping others, and the routine of working in a rich man's household seemed not to define her in the least. It added nothing to her, nor did it detract from her sense of self or calling. This explained why she preferred the Army to participation in local churches. She clearly determined to act out her faith rather than to sing it or testify to it in any of the local ecclesiastical expressions.

I can't recall when she first approached me about college. It was probably in the early months of my senior year in high school. She felt strongly that I should go to college, and in this she differed radically from the advice offered by Mrs. Bunch. They worked in the same household, but I am not sure they were close friends. Mrs. Bunch had suggested that I consider enlisting in the military. I couldn't imagine doing that, nor why she would even suggest it. My guess, looking back on it, was her fear that I would get some local girl "in the family way," as it was expressed in those days, and would have to get married and settle down in that small, going-nowhere town.

In the months that followed, Mildred would inform me of her attempts to raise money from local churches to get me launched into college. She had been encouraged at first by a local pastor whose congregation seemed to be the most prosperous in town. I knew some of their parishioners from my caddying days at the country club. But this pastor expressed only mild interest in supporting entry into a school that was not in line with his understanding of the Christian faith.

His understanding and Mildred's were far apart. He initially thought that maybe "two years at a Bible school might be all right, but certainly not four years." His final recommendation of a four-year liberal arts church-related college did not suit her. And that was the end of that. I suspect that she was also put off by his lack of focus on the gospel in his preaching. He was a gifted speaker with a presence and demeanor that were calculated to please his upper-class parishioners, but no one would associate him with biblical preaching of a more evangelical nature.

The pastor of the Missionary Church recommended a Bible college in Fort Wayne, Indiana. It was the college that grew out of the mission of the Missionary Church Association, the denomination of which the congregation was a part. A. D. Randall was my pastor, and, except for the fact that his sons had attended the school, I had never heard of it and scarcely knew where Fort Wayne was.

Mildred had contacted him for counsel and support. Mr. Randall shared her interest in my attending Bible college. I asked him why I should do so since I knew nothing about the Bible. He smiled his warmest pastoral smile and suggested that that was possibly a good reason to go. Mildred apparently agreed, and on a hot day in the spring of 1947 she presented me with five hundred dollars of her own money, assuring me that "we ought to strike while the iron is hot." With this money, I embarked on a Bible college education.

9

Fort Wayne Bible College

ON A FALL DAY in 1947 I walked up the eleven steps into Founders Hall of what was then the Fort Wayne Bible Institute. It was called an institute, but I had no idea what the term meant.

The Bible Institute was located in one of the loveliest and wealthiest residential areas in Fort Wayne. The neighborhood was blessed with beautiful tree-lined streets and more-than-adequate transportation to assure that getting in and out of the shopping areas downtown would be most accommodating. Without knowing it, I was about to be trained to go into all the world from a rather lush setting in suburbia.

I dropped my luggage and walked into the hallway where I was greeted by Jared F. Gerig, the dean of students. He welcomed me warmly.

After a brief conversation, he suggested I might like to room with an upperclassman. Then he told me that the person was a Negro. I suppose he assumed that the person he had in mind would be compatible with me and could possibly introduce me to the routines of institute life. He was right and he was wrong.

Tom Florence was born in 1918 in the home of a sharecropper family ten miles from Greensboro, North Carolina. His father was a hard-working farmer who was part of a black community that was hardly making it. Tom admitted to being timid of spirit with an inferiority complex. He assigned the reason for this to the discrimination that bedeviled his early life. All the systems that set the perimeters of his life told him that he was nothing. But his family was deeply committed to following Jesus. His father was a preacher, as had been his grandfather. Tom was converted when he was eleven years old. His early passion was to know Jesus and to make him known to others.

After high school he was drafted into the Army, eventually serving in New Guinea and Guadalcanal. After four years, at the end of the war, he sought a place where he could study the Bible. Upon the recommendation of a white believer, he chose Fort Wayne Bible Institute.

He arrived by taxi, full of both anxiety and hope. He was met on the steps of Shultz Hall by several white students who lifted his heavy luggage, carried it into the building that would be his home, and left behind a surprised and happy twenty-eight-year-old black student, convinced that God had led him to this place. He had never had any white person carry his luggage before.

I arrived at those same steps fresh out of high school. I was light complexioned and from Michigan. I had been a Christian a little over one year. We had no segregated drinking fountains in our town, no social rituals that reminded people of color that they were inferior. I did not come to Bible school with an inferiority complex. It would take the administration a while to recognize the significance of the difference between Tom and me. By the time they did, it would be that same dean who would admonish me about not getting too friendly with the girls on campus. There were hardly any non-white girls there.

My new roommate walked me down the hall from our room. He had become acclimated to the place and began to introduce me to the guys. One of them invited me in. I was struck by the books in his room. I asked if they were from his classes or the library and he told me, no, they were his. I had never seen so many books belonging to one person. We had no such collection where I was raised, and neither did any of my friends.

Thus began my love affair with books. Not only could I read them; I could also possess them, make them my own. I could go back to them years later.

Tom also introduced me to work detail. It was the school's policy to assign all students a detail, an area we would clean each day. We would be granted a sum of money for this, to be applied to our tuition.

Tom, having been there a year ahead of me, had been assigned the men's room, and I was assigned to the same area. We did latrines, toilets, and shower stalls. Tom was more accepting of this than I was. His spiritual life was much more attuned to the disciplines of servanthood than mine. I knew I was saved, but I didn't know that I was saved to serve. And certainly not in a latrine. A couple of years later a new student up from Jamaica would refuse to do this work. He said it was "for niggers."

My classmates were white, as were all my professors. Tom and I were the only black students. We couldn't know this at the time, but we would be the only full-time black students there throughout our years in attendance. Our classmates were there to prepare for Christian service, and they seemed to know how you did that. At least they came from the kinds of churches and associations that featured that activity as its reason to be.

All the models for these activities were white, male and female. In addition to our studies, we would attend daily chapel. And every Friday evening, we would attend Mission Band, where we would be exposed to visiting missionaries and to the dire spiritual conditions of the regions beyond.

Each semester we would listen to outstanding speakers whose purpose was to undergird the school's deep commitment to our spiritual life. This life was defined as sanctification, a so-called second work of grace. We were expected to respond, even if we didn't walk down the aisle to kneel at the altar.

I was usually impressed with the speakers. By the time we were seniors, we had listened to some remarkable individuals. These included A. W. Tozer, whose 1948 book *The Pursuit of God* had made him a household name among evangelicals, and Andrew Blackwood, who taught preaching at Princeton Theological Seminary.

Our president, Safara A. Witmer, and Dean Gerig were also excellent speakers. They taught the theory of sanctification, but it never took for me. Something was missing, and I didn't know what. During my senior year, a Baptist preacher whose two sons were classmates preached in chapel, and that was when I first learned what it was that had been missing: grace.

In the four years I attended the school, I felt deeply the absence of non-white speakers at any of these events. Nor were there any non-white missionaries or evangelists.

There was another aspect of the holiness tradition about which we were ignorant. It was the relationship between holiness and social reform. Surely our faculty knew about the revivals led by nineteenth-century evangelist Charles Finney or the leadership of Mrs. Phoebe Palmer among the Methodists. The school was part of the holiness tradition, whose emphasis was the sanctification of believers and a life of holiness. It was called by different names, I was to learn later: the deeper life, holiness, the Spirit-filled life, and so on.

The roots of these movements were deeply embedded in all major denominations and were especially prominent in the American church's attempt to reform the nation after the Civil War. This was especially the case in ministries among the poor in the key cities of the country. It was the holiness movement that gave birth to the Salvation Army and to rescue missions in English and American cities.

Without realizing it, we were becoming fundamentalists. No one recruited us, and we took no courses in the topic. It was in the air and was often the topic of scuttlebutt discussions in the dorm. Yet these discussions often devolved into questions regarding a person's eternal security and how a believer was to behave in public. Or, to put it another way, how much "public" was a believer to appropriate in the course of a night on the town?

Fundamentalism seemed to be a cure for worldliness. But no one informed us that it was fundamentalism that had sustained the American evangelical traditions after the Civil War. No one helped to shape our awareness of fundamentalism as the foundation of all the evangelical seminaries and Bible colleges in America.

For someone as green as I, this was more than an unfortunate omission. I needed to know this history if I was to find myself as part of a movement that had meaning beyond Sunday school, evangelism, and missions. On the other hand, what would I have thought or done with fundamentalism's importance to the evangelical movement when I realized that it was almost entirely a whites-only network of powerful churches and Bible colleges? Just like the one I attended.

At this particular moment there were peculiar stirrings among fundamentalists, but we didn't know it. Even had we known about these stirrings, they would not have included Tom and me.

Awakenings among white groups rarely included black Christians. When they did, black people tended to be the objects of revivalist endeavors. We were not expected to participate. During these years neither Harold Ockenga, pastor of the prominent Park Street Church in Boston, who helped found Fuller Seminary in 1947, nor Carl F. H. Henry, evangelical theologian and author of *The Uneasy Conscience of Modern Fundamentalism*, could find a way to include non-white evangelicals in all their work or writings. We had never heard of Walter Rauschenbusch and his classic *A Theology for the Social Gospel*.

At the heart of the debates among fundamentalists and modernists was the issue of the humanity of Jesus. We were taught that he was born of a virgin and was therefore the Son of God. It seemed to be the bedrock of our theology. But the liberals seemed to have stolen the limelight in the culture by an emphasis upon his humanity. It was a short leap from this emphasis to a definition of ministry as social ministry.

Ockenga and his evangelical colleagues in New England began to find better ways to reclaim the American church and culture from the "liberals," who we heard had control of the World Council of Churches. Their efforts would eventually culminate in the National Association of Evangelicals. We would not study the historical relationship between the gospel and culture that made up the history of Western civilization. But then we were a Bible college, not a seminary. I didn't know the difference because I had never heard the word "seminary."

In both camps the battle was over finding an identity from which influence and power could be wielded in the struggle for religious control over the hearts and minds of Americans. Among evangelicals there were as many mistaken notions of the social gospel as were present among liberals regarding evangelicals and fundamentalists. At this time the drama was being played out mostly in the eastern parts of the country, from Boston to Philadelphia. We were in Indiana.

Yet there were other stirrings in the culture about which we were ignorant. These stirrings were in the South and were being led by people we would not learn about until a decade had passed.

One other thing I didn't know until later was that during my freshman year a new seminary was being launched in California. One of its purposes was to reform fundamentalism.

Another development that would have a profound effect on all of us was the emergence of a movement aimed at reaching the world's young people. It was called Youth for Christ. It was an urban ministry, and its first full-time evangelist was a young man fresh out of Wheaton College and a local pastorate. His name was Billy Graham.

We had no knowledge of South Africa and the establishment of apartheid as the official doctrine of segregation in 1947. We certainly had no knowledge of a black pastor in South Carolina who had sued a white school board for discrimination against his children by denying them their rights to equal protection as guaranteed by the Constitution. That suit, as it waddled its way through the legal system all the way to the Supreme Court as *Brown v. Board of Education of Topeka*, would forever change the face of public education in the United States. No one mentioned it at our Bible college.

The absence of a curriculum to better serve the needs of students called to evangelize the world weighed heavily on the mind of the school's president. He seemed to me to be distant and aloof from the faculty and student body. There were rumors that faculty meetings were not always characterized by good will. He was an intellectual and a visionary. He was also a former officer in the Army. Years later I would learn that during my years at the school, President Witmer was deeply involved in discussions about the need for a new association of schools that would expose students to a more rigorous academic course of study, one that would enable them to compete with their secular counterparts.

A new organization was soon created to achieve these goals. It was called the Accrediting Association of Bible Institutes and Bible Colleges (now the Association for Biblical Higher Education). President Witmer, often known as "Mr. Bible College," would become its first president. In 1950 our school changed its name to the Fort Wayne Bible College.

As early as 1955, a strong part of the bachelor of arts curriculum at Fort Wayne was a four-year pre-seminary program. But neither reformation nor urban youth ministry was in our curriculum. Reformation, I was to learn later, required more intellectual acumen and acuity than we were exposed to. After all, if your sole purpose was the evangelization of the world before the second coming of Jesus, the curriculum could be more practical than prophetic, more personal than social. The world we were sent to evangelize was a forbidding place, a landscape dotted with land mines. We received very little help in locating those mines, let alone in understanding who placed them there.

The country was slowly emerging from a global conflict. Most people were fully supportive of war efforts but tired of war. The economy was wheezing its way back to productivity: Fords and Chevys in Detroit, beans in Boston, Dinah Shore urging Americans to see the USA in a Chevrolet, new housing for veterans in what would become the locus of the American dream, the suburbs. Levittown, where all the houses were made of ticky-tacky, and all looked the same, as one songwriter put it.

Storm clouds were taking shape on distant horizons. They would become clearer during the fifties, and the issues that would emerge would forever change the way Christians would define themselves and their identity as Americans.

I'm not certain when I realized that I could think, that I could become a good student. I didn't start out with that awareness. I was certain that I was in the wrong place when I first opened my Greek textbook. There was no way that what I saw could be understood. What silliness. Surely these folks could not be serious. They were, and they argued that since the New Testament was written in Greek, no education would be respectable if it did not take that language seriously. Besides, it was in the curriculum.

The teacher didn't help. She was elderly and looked like an original Greek. She was one of the veteran faculty members, maybe an original member. It took me most of the year to realize that I was wrong about her. I went to her office one day to confess my feelings. She took me by the arm, and we walked down the hall as she seemed to become more of a mother than a professor of Greek. She became one of my favorites.

I was also wrong about my ability to learn the Greek texts. It may have been in that class that I began to believe that I could think. I gained further confidence in the dorm rooms where we would gather in preparation for an exam. I had become a pretty good student without knowing it, although I would never win the school's trophy as a valedictorian. It would take several years beyond Bible college for me to realize that I was calling people to repent about stuff that God wasn't especially interested in.

I was exposed to culture with my first hearing of Handel's *Messiah*. The famous oratorio was the capstone of the fall semester and heralded the celebration of the Christmas season. I had never heard of it but was encouraged to attend.

I wasn't impressed. Too highfalutin for my taste. But that very evening a group of students invited me to go with them to a neighboring city to hear it again. Berne, Indiana, was a small town south of Fort Wayne, and the oratorio was an annual event. While it was sung in the sanctuary of a Mennonite church, it had taken on the aura of a civic event. I was pleased to accept the invitation because it would at least get me out of town for an evening.

In that sanctuary, I first felt what that piece of classical music could offer. I felt there was something more to this college experience than studies and preparations for ministry. I began to experience the gentle stirrings of a culture with which I was not familiar. I had missed it in high school when I had the lead part in *Our Town*.

I don't recall hearing anyone argue about dating on campus. Girls were probably the majority of the student body, and by now us guys knew that girls were here to stay. No one in chapel preached from the text where God declares that it is not good for a man to be alone.

Tom and I talked about the issue of dating and knew that the deck was stacked against us. The rules were clear; one could date only those within one's own race. Nevertheless, we did identify the ladies we could get serious about if . . . Tom had as good an eye as I, but he was no real threat to the system. He had vowed, years before coming to the school, that he would never marry a white woman.

I had never made such a vow, but my early experience with the parents of white girls in high school convinced me this was not a likely option. I seemed to be more of a threat to the system than Tom—lighter complexion, younger, more culturally attuned to the white majority. Culturally, I was more white than black.

But I was colored—and in the eyes of the administration, that was enough. I do not recall any incident. It may have been simply that I was getting too friendly with girls in general. Or the dean may have received a request from the dean of women that I be counseled. Anyhow, I found myself sitting across the desk from the dean, hearing him remind me of the rules and asking me to "lay off" the girls. It was a strange admonition. Not a conversation, but a one-way caution, a shot across the bow even though the shell was small bore.

Years later, this same man, by then the president of the National Association of Evangelicals as well as the president of the college, learned that I had been invited to preach in chapel. He sent a request that I not mention the civil rights movement or such issues related to politics.

I agreed to comply and took my sermon topic from the theme of the association for that year: "The Evangelical Imperative—World in Crisis, the Church Involved." The theme itself was enough to expose the silliness of his request. And it made my sermon an easy exercise in reminding the students that an evangelical imperative is found in an allegiance to Jesus and his love of the world.

Sometime in my sophomore year I met Eleanor Lyon. She was a year ahead of me, so I recall having no classes with her. Indeed, I don't remember now how we met.

I invited her to an event in which I was to be recognized. We sat together at dinner. I was nervous. I had not dated anyone since high school.

Eleanor was a Native American. Her mother was full-blooded, her father white. She was from Ohio. She was studying to be a missionary to her American tribal counterparts.

We began to exchange letters. When one was perfumed, I knew there was something going on that was serious. We worked together on campus events. She was a fine artist, and the images of her version of Sallman's head of Christ adorned most of the campus art events. We sang together in the school's League of Nations Gospel Team.

Eleanor graduated a year ahead of me, and by that time our classmates assumed that we were set for life. I may have thought so also, as we retained our relationship, our love affair really, during the early years of ministry beyond Bible college.

In the spring of 1951, I stood in front of Founders Memorial Hall with my "paper" in hand. I graduated.

PART 2

Evangelism: 1951–1974

10

Coming Home

In 1951, as I stood in front of Founders Memorial Hall to receive my diploma from Fort Wayne Bible College, the early summer afternoon was bathed in sunlight. Aunt Edna attended the graduation. We both wondered what was next.

The next day, my classmate Gerald Gerig and I left for Dodge City, Kansas, in his car. Dodge City, for the record, was not the town that Errol Flynn put to rest in the 1939 Western movie by that title.

I enjoyed the week. I led singing, did some solo work, listened to Gerald preach, and played golf on a public course whose "greens" were made of dirt.

On our way back to Fort Wayne, we stopped in Wichita for a brief ministry at a local Methodist church. When we arrived back in Fort Wayne, Gerald dropped me off in front of the same building from which I had graduated two weeks before. I went to the business office to pay my bill. I had graduated from Bible college with the huge debt of three hundred dollars.

While standing in front of Founders Hall, I heard someone call my name. I looked up and saw Fred Millikan coming across the street. Fred, an older man, had been very helpful during my years in college, especially when I seemed lost. I had borrowed shirts from him. He asked if I was busy. The twinkle in his eye told me he already knew the answer to his question. He then told me that a city-wide camp meeting was being held in Elkton, Michigan, one hundred miles north of Detroit, and asked if I would be available. They needed a song leader. I told him I was available but that I had no transportation. Fred took me to a local Greyhound station, and I spent the entire day traveling from Fort Wayne to Elkton.

The meetings in Elkton went well and I enjoyed the company of Blanchard Amstutz, also a graduate of Fort Wayne Bible College, and his wife. They were part of the musical team. The two weeks went rather quickly. Blanchard asked me what I was going to do next. I told him I was going home.

He then invited me to accompany him and his family to their next assignment, a camp meeting in Wren, Ohio. I had been there before as a member of a Bible college team visiting one of the churches. A classmate was from there. I agreed to go. Blanchard assured me that I could sing and maybe lead the children's session. And besides, he assured me, this is how you get exposure that will lead to other meetings. He was right.

I was listed in the fine print of the program as "Associate Singer and Child Entertainer." Frank Norris, popular in the Midwest, was the evangelist. We would work together several times in the area, including a major countywide effort in Van Wert, Ohio, where I served as soloist and song leader. In most of these meetings in this area, I stayed with Pearl and Bob Robey. We enjoyed a mutual love of preaching and sport cars.

Over the next few years, I sang and preached in churches near Van Wert: Evangelical United Brethren, Methodist, United Brethren, Friends. These churches were part of the farm communities of upper northern Ohio. I worked an occasional meeting in similar settings in Michigan.

In these gatherings I was the only non-white person. Black people were not farmers, in my experience. Furthermore, some, if not most, of these communities had unspoken "understandings" about colored people living in their midst. Not all of these towns had such understandings or ordinances, but it was well known that black people were not welcome after dark in those that did.

I was not aware of these attitudes and behaviors, and no one mentioned them. Only years later, when such behaviors became embarrassing, did a fuller story emerge. In the meantime, I stayed in the homes of members. I usually liked that, especially if there were children present.

During one of the most important revival meetings in northern Ohio, I stayed in the home of a local farmer and his family. Howard Cryer and his wife, Ilo, had two boys. Their home was warm in temperature and spirit.

When the boys bounded off the school bus, we would sit in front of their TV set and watch *Howdy Doody*.

That particular evangelistic series lasted two weeks. During the second week, Ilo came to me and announced that she and her husband had decided that I needed a car. I was stunned. She asked if I had any money. I told her that I had five hundred dollars—maybe. She then told me that they would give me the rest.

The next day we drove into nearby Montpelier and bought a brand new 1962 four-door Chevrolet. What an enormous gift. No more bus stations; freedom between meetings; even freedom to visit home. They told me to pay them back when I got it, or if not, to forget it. The relationship with the Cryers lasted for many years. They came to our wedding. I visited them on trips across the area in subsequent years. I saw their boys, now grown, inherit the farm. I knew they would be good farmers like their parents. I did pay them back.

Over the ensuing months I led the music and preached in churches across this part of northern Ohio. When I had some time off, or just needed a place to sleep, I would stop with another white family, this time the home of my old friend Howard Dunlap. I knew Howard from our Bible college days. He was one year ahead of me. Howard and his wife, Ruth, served two congregations near Montpelier. They shuttled their pastoral energies between churches in exotic communities with names like Cooney. The denomination called itself Christian Union, and I held revival meetings in several of its churches in Ohio. I led the singing, told children's stories, and sang solos at revival meetings. They always treated me as a member of the family.

It was this long-standing relationship that made it easy for me to invite myself to lunch when I learned that a well-known preacher from Detroit was to be the guest speaker at Howard's church. I had heard about B. M. Nottage for years. He and his brother T. B. were regular preachers at the Assembly in my hometown of Sturgis. I had met T. B. but not B. M. Howard assured me that I would be welcome.

It was a meeting that would begin the most important transition in my adult life. "Bill," he said, "it is nice that you enjoy the friendship and ministry among our white friends, but we need you too." Nottage then invited me to visit Detroit. What I didn't know was that my sister Beverly had told him about me on one of her visits to Detroit. I agreed, and in the next week received an invitation to join him and his family for dinner in the Motor City.

I drove my new Chevy across the south end of Detroit and thought about my early exposure to the city. During high school, some of my friends and I had gone to the city to see the Detroit Tigers play. The walk from the Greyhound station out to Briggs Stadium was a long one. (The name would later be changed to Tiger Stadium.)

In the early fifties the city became for me a lovely metropolis of boulevards, parks, and stately homes. This was the Motor City where Ford, Chrysler, and General Motors slugged it out for supremacy in the hearts, minds, and pocketbooks of Americans in love with their automobiles.

The city was anchored at the south end of Woodward Avenue, the main thoroughfare that divided the city east and west. A new city hall had been dedicated, and it was fronted by an impressive statue, created by American sculptor Marshall Fredericks, and named The Spirit of Detroit. Years later I would read the signature sentence at the base of that statue that was to serve as the city's commitment to civic harmony. It read: "Now the Lord is that Spirit, and where the Spirit of the Lord is, there is liberty." Over the next few years, I was to learn that hardly anyone in the city's leadership knew about that famous verse from the Bible. Or if so, did not know how to work with it in civic life. Neither did the leadership of the city's churches.

I arrived at the Nottage home on the city's east side in good time for dinner. I was impressed that a man of his reputation would live in such an inconspicuous house. Pastor Nottage and his wife, Leah, welcomed me and introduced me to other guests present. Wednesday was the day his secretary came to the house to assist him with his correspondence. Her name was Hazel Scott.

I was pleased to accept their invitation to stay in their home for the night. The next day was traveling day, but before I left, Mr. Nottage asked me if I knew what the Lord was doing these days. When I replied that he was saving people from their sins through the gospel, he replied that that was what God had always been doing. And that led him to the text in Acts 15 where James reminded the elders of the church that God chose a people from among the nations who should bear his name. It was clear that this was a foundational text for Nottage. I had not heard this passage used in this manner and had not preached from it. But this was my introduction to what would be several years of listening to Nottage expound on the church as the people of God.

The issue at hand in this passage was the legitimacy of the gentile experience of grace and the Holy Spirit. It became clear in the years ahead that this was also the jumping-off text from which Nottage preached the gospel to the black community. From here he moved easily to Ephesians and Colossians to argue that God was no respecter of persons. White people might be, including those who called themselves believers, but God was inclusive. And black believers were near, so very near to God, that in the person of his Son, they were as near as he.

I gradually fell in love with Detroit. Between revival meetings I would point my Chevy toward the city and the Nottage residence on Belvidere Street. Mrs. Nottage welcomed me as a frequent guest. It was in this home that I first caught a glimpse of the possibility that marriage could still be alive after forty years. I began to feel connected there as if a part of a new family.

At this time, I had a conversation with the president of the Missionary Church Association. We met in his office in Fort Wayne. Dr. Safara Witmer had served as the dean of the college, its president, and was now head of the denomination.

He received me warmly. I was not surprised. I had always respected the man and liked him as a person. I was certain that the feeling was mutual. I recited my movements and how I had found a home among churches in Detroit. He was pleased and relieved. He admitted that he knew of no openings within the association.

I don't think I was surprised about this last part. Looking back on that conversation, I knew, whether I wanted to admit it or not, that my hopes and dreams were beyond either expectation or desire for such a relationship. I should have known, after all the years of exposure to the denomination and the college, that there would be no place for me, or any black graduates, in these associations.

Now, for the first time, I was in the company of black believers—a whole network of them, an entire city full of people who looked like me. It was as if I was coming home after years in some sort of exile.

11

Pleased to Be Part of Something New

IN THE EARLY FIFTIES I had a rather busy evangelistic schedule. Ever enthusiastic, I knew I had much to learn. The 1950s would become learning years, often in places and with people that surprised me.

I pointed my new Chevy in the direction of Iowa, where I preached in a small congregation of Christian Union saints. In Iowa I submitted my absentee vote for Dwight Eisenhower as the Republican candidate for president in 1952. I enjoyed the place and its people.

But I was glad to head back to Detroit. There was a network of Plymouth Brethren Assemblies there that stretched from central Detroit to River Rouge, from mid-city to Eight Mile to the north. There were seven of these congregations.

Beyond Detroit there were similar gatherings of Christians in Assemblies in Cleveland and Terre Haute, across the state in Muskegon, and in Chicago. All of these gatherings of African American believers traced their foundations to the influence of B. M. and T. B. Nottage. Because of the Nottages, over the next several years I was welcomed in all these centers.

I was not the only young evangelist drawn to the Nottage residence. The most influential of these men was T. Michael Flowers. Michael carried himself with a confident air. A powerful preacher, well educated in theology, he had a passion to evangelize in the black communities of America.

Mrs. Nottage, with the assistance of Sister Scott from the church, would feed and care for them all. Michael would endear himself to the Nottage household by courting and marrying one of their daughters. They seemed to have had three such young women—"daughters" as they were called. Shermine married my old college roommate, Tom Florence. Ella married Michael. And Hazel married me.

My relationship with Mr. Nottage became special. I had begun to see him as the kind of father I wish I could have had. He, in turn, seemed to relate to me in a different manner than he did with these other men. This climaxed when he gave me the key to his house. This bothered his secretary. She had been a part of this household longer than I but did not have such a key.

As our relationship matured, I became his chauffeur. We would visit several rescue missions in the city, collecting leftover foodstuffs and delivering them to the elderly and shut-ins of the congregation. I became acquainted with poor members of the congregations as well and was impressed with the love they had for him.

I also became acquainted with the network of white evangelicals who shared their resources and networks of influence with Nottage. I began to circulate among this network, which came to include the local chapter of the Evangelical Association, the Detroit Bible Institute, and leaders of the local chapter of InterVarsity Christian Fellowship at nearby Wayne State University.

Nottage was connected to this network of evangelicals in Detroit. He could drive his car in the city, but it was on the longer trips when an aging Nottage needed help. He was recovering from a heart attack, so in addition to his well-worn Bible, he carried his pills. The latter were courtesy of Mrs. Nottage, who wouldn't let him out of the house without them.

These trips out of state—to Cleveland, Philadelphia, and New York City—were like seminars to me. I was the chauffeur to the bishop of these churches, and he seemed to relish an opportunity to disciple a young preacher in Pauline theology as it centered on the "mystery" of the church. Mr. Nottage was evangelical in theology, but not in culture. He knew, as we all did, that evangelical culture was white. In culture, he remained a loving and grateful son of the Bahamian Islands.

The preachers he most respected were those he listened to on the radio—M. R. DeHaan and his Radio Bible Class and Donald Grey Barnhouse, minister of the Tenth Presbyterian Church in Philadelphia—and conversations with his friends at *Eternity* magazine and at *Our Hope* magazine, edited by Arno C. Gaebelein. These were voices from a fading fundamentalism and Plymouth Brethren influence. I was a total stranger to this tradition, although I did enjoy Barnhouse's style of Bible teaching.

The legacy of B. M. Nottage centered on his passion to expose black Americans to the gospel. He was an evangelist in heart and talent. He was also a churchman who either founded or was the midwife at the births of congregations from Detroit to St. Louis, Terre Haute, and Chicago. By the time of his death in 1972, not only were there six or seven congregations in Detroit that he had had a hand in, but across the country there were hundreds of young men and women who had been discipled by him in the Scriptures. He was influential in establishing two Bible camps in Michigan. The chapel at Cedine Bible Camp in Tennessee bears his name.

Nottage was totally unselfish in encouraging young men to pursue their sense of calling to the ministry, and there was no attempt on his part to bind their callings to himself. I recall a letter that reached him at his home. It was from a student from Fuller Seminary in Pasadena. After he read it, he handed it to me. The student was a Negro, and he expressed his concern that black leaders had no organization into which they could express their concerns and mutual support. What was needed, he wrote, was something like the National Association of Evangelicals that had served white Christian leaders so well. He asked for Nottage's advice.

I was impressed, as was Nottage, and in typical fashion he sent the student an encouraging reply. The young man was Marvin Prentis, and he became the leading architect of the National Negro Evangelical Association (now the National Black Evangelical Association), which had its inaugural meeting in Los Angeles in 1963.

The other aspect of his legacy was his willingness to pursue fellowship with white believers, especially those in nearby Plymouth Brethren churches. White believers had been present at the beginning of his ministry in those tent meetings in Black Bottom. As congregations began to develop, a goodly number of these believers continued to follow his preaching. I was impressed as I noticed that no important event in the life of the black Assemblies would be without white believers in the audience and on the platform as speakers. His rationale for this inclusion was his understanding of the church as the body of Christ. He refused to allow white reluctance to follow through on the same premise to deter his practice. This commitment was tested during the mid-fifties through the mid-sixties as, one by one, white Assemblies abandoned Detroit for the more comfortable confines of suburbia. I was inclined to write them off. After all, if they did not desire our fellowship, I felt they were the losers. Let 'em go!

Nottage was not of this mind. He was prepared to be true to the Scriptures and the Spirit of Christ. He would pursue the saints wherever he found them. I thought such an exercise was a waste of time. B. M. was wiser than me. He knew that white believers had deeper pockets and that when they sold their church buildings, they would offer them to us first. This was important, for Detroit was changing. New freeways had divided the city, and old Detroit businesses that had anchored the area were moving to the suburbs. The core of the city had aged. Newness was the agenda. Black people were not included in plans for a new Detroit, but old neighborhoods were opening, and new congregations were vying for new buildings.

Bethany Tabernacle was one of those congregations. For them, it was move or die. Nottage would not accept a salary from Bethany. The congregation did share love offerings with him, but he was reluctant to accept anything more because he felt they couldn't afford it.

His hero was George Müller, one of the founders of the Plymouth Brethren movement in England. It was Müller who also started the orphanage movement in Great Britain. I had not heard of Müller, but it was clear that if Nottage had a hero, Müller was it. It was the Englishman's attitude toward money and its usage that attracted Nottage. Support for ministry, according to the English leader, came from prayer, asking and receiving, and putting one's needs before Jesus, who said that "whatsoever ye shall ask in my name, that will I do" (John 14:13 KJV). Müller based all his work upon this text. And as God gave to him, he in turn would give to those whom he served, especially orphans and the poor.

I gradually came to see how radical this attitude and practice was. I also began to understand how B. M. and Leah could be so content in their humble home. I became aware that Nottage always included a small check in his correspondence with missionaries or others engaged in ministry locally. It wasn't much, but it was something. He received, and therefore he gave. Vintage Müller.

There were other fish to fry: the need to reach young people. I was pleased to be a part of something new. It was the tradition among the older leaders to reserve Saturday night for young people at the annual Bible conferences. These were held in Detroit and Cleveland. I became a part of the leadership of this group. In between conferences we would have Saturday night rallies, not unlike those held by the local Detroit area Youth for Christ movement.

We were not part of Youth for Christ planning even though we were in Detroit. YFC was a white organization, an organization that emphasized rallies for young people across the nation. I was personally acquainted with the leader of the organization in Detroit, but it was clear that we were "included out" of his plans. So I decided to learn from his programming and take it back to our young people.

Our youth meetings grew, and it was clear that we needed to expand. We took our concern to Nottage, and he gave us his blessing. Our vision was to have an annual youth conference, a weekend in the tri-state area that would draw young people from Cleveland to Chicago. I was part of a small delegation that motored to Battle Creek and the Kellogg Foundation. We were graciously received, and we signed on to host a weekend conference at their center. Thus began what became the most successful annual youth conference in the history of these black Assemblies. The conference was eventually forced to relocate because it had outgrown the Kellogg site.

The success of these gatherings may have spelled the end of the old order of black Assembly life. The young adults that filled leadership roles throughout the late fifties and early sixties were college bound and headed for professions that opened the world to them. They became aware of the cultural significance of the black church and the broader importance of black institutions—and in the distance, a cloud that was the emergence of the civil rights movement.

12

"When Did You Know That You Loved Me?"

It was the fall of 2021. Hazel and I had been married sixty-six years. I was preparing her for bed. It had become something of a ritual. As her health continued to decline, she would not always be lucid in her speech. I had worked my way to her feet, and she broke the silence with a question. "When did you know that you loved me?"

I was caught off guard. Was this another off-the-wall question, as she would sometimes utter? Or was she serious?

She was serious. I couldn't come up with a quick answer, and by the time I made a stab at it, she was on to something else. Another part of her aching body needed attention. I tucked her in, read the Scriptures, and before prayer, she was asleep.

I still cannot recall when I first knew I loved Hazel, but I knew where it all began. I had reached the tender age of twenty-three. I was dating a fine Christian woman from among the young people of the Assemblies. She was serious, and I enjoyed her company, but I was not inclined to marry her. She was confident, she told me, that I would come around to it. I didn't. But maybe it was time to get serious about marriage.

I knew I would have little difficulty in finding a woman for such an adventure. After all, there were always more girls than boys in the churches. I knew that I was one of the more eligible bachelors in our Assembly network. And beyond. What to do?

I decided to pray about it. Maybe I had prayed before in general terms, but this time, I seemed to be smart enough to know what I needed in a wife. So, I knelt at the bedside in the bedroom at the Nottages' house and laid my thoughts before the Lord. "I am too dumb to make such a choice. So please take over this part of my life, will you?" And I really meant it. I got up from that bedside knowing that something had been settled.

I had no clue that the person would be Hazel Scott. Hazel was living with her sister. Doris Rayford was married and the mother of three children. Like many black women new to the cities of the North, Doris plied her craft as a nurse's assistant, which is a euphemism for someone who does the dirty work on the floor and in the laundry room. She, like the other sisters of the family, had migrated from their home in Memphis. Their father had left the home to pursue the favors of a woman who was not their mother, and to find work that would support his family of four. One by one, they followed him to Chicago and then to Detroit.

Hazel enrolled in a small business college, intending to become a stenographer. She secured a job at the Detroit Orthopedic Center. She pursued her interest in church and attended a flagship congregation of the African American churches in greater Detroit.

But it was an encounter with a white girl that changed her life. She invited Hazel to a meeting of young people associated with InterVarsity Christian Fellowship. It was there that Hazel heard the gospel message and was led to faith in Christ by the young lady.

That same woman was also a member of the network of Plymouth Brethren churches, and she introduced Hazel to Bethany Tabernacle, whose pastor was B. M. Nottage. Nottage and his wife, Leah, welcomed her into their own household, and she became one of their "daughters." We were friends and worked together in youth ministry among the churches.

When I left town for evangelistic meetings, I would leave my Chevy with her. She was living with her sister, and I knew that she was getting tired of that arrangement. Too many kids, too little space. So when she told me that she was planning to buy a house, I was impressed. It sounded like something she would do, and could do. Besides, she wasn't getting any younger, crowding thirty. She had finally located a house on Detroit's west side and informed me of the arrangements to make her first payment with the realtor and the owner. I offered to drive her, and she accepted. She was nervous. The transaction went smoothly. She agreed to purchase the house for $13,582 dollars, and Mrs. Grace Cole, the owner, agreed to payments of $100 per month. We drove away.

Hazel was pleased but a bit overwhelmed. She had done it, and there was no turning back. She was a house owner. I was impressed since she was the only young, single woman I knew who had the gumption to buy a house before she was thirty. I had no idea that I would end up moving into the same house less than two years later.

Back to her question. Had she been awake and alert, I would have reminded her of our trip back from the annual Bible conference in Cleveland in 1954. We had arrived separately, but I asked her if she would like to ride with me back to Detroit. She agreed. She apparently enjoyed the ride, and I was pleased with her company. We arrived at her house on Colfax that she shared with her oldest sister.

We parked in her driveway and began a conversation that ended with our holding hands. Something was going on between us and we knew it. We kissed, one of those nice kisses that said thanks for a lovely time. But we knew something else was going on.

I knew I was in trouble. Hazel was not one to mess with. If what I was feeling was for real, that was one thing; if not, I had better call it off quick. I mentioned my interest in Hazel to Pastor Nottage. He was quiet and pastoral. He noted that she was older than me. Almost five years older. I was surprised and a bit stunned. An older woman? Marry a woman that much older than me?

But I knew that she was different. She didn't play the piano or lead the choir. She didn't even sing in the choir. She was mature and all woman. I sensed the hand of God in this budding relationship. The next time we embraced, it was not casual. We soon enjoyed a kissing relationship. I was in love. Even her older sister knew she was in love with "that young man." In a little over a year, we were married.

I knew that I wanted to present Hazel with a nice engagement ring, and I knew where I'd like to buy one. So on my way back to Detroit from a meeting in Indiana, I stopped in Sturgis and entered Mr. Griffith's shop. He was pleased to see me and very happy to learn of my engagement, and that I was engaged to one of Mr. Nottage's daughters.

Anticipating my request for a suitable ring, he walked me to his cabinet and retrieved an attractive unit. I was dazzled by its beauty. He would accept no payment. I floated from his shop, got in the Chevy, and pointed toward Detroit. The next evening as Hazel and I stood before her fireplace in the living room, I presented her with an engagement ring. She was very pleased.

From kindergarten to that day, Mr. Griffith had been God's agent to stand by the door, to watch over me, to see that I got where the Spirit wanted me to be.

Hazel didn't want to hear all of that when she asked the question, "When did you know that you loved me?" There was another question that never got asked in her presence, one that had haunted me for some time. It might have been asked by the other woman I thought I loved. Eleanor Lyon might have asked, "Why didn't you love me?" I never knew the answer. I thought I did love her, and I had thought, as I'm certain she did also, that we would marry. I was keeping company with her as I was getting acquainted with the churches in Detroit. She was a classy woman, elegant in manners, stylish in dress. She was an artist, played piano, and knew her way around a kitchen. I knew that we could marry. Why didn't it happen? It had everything to do with that prayer I made in Mrs. Nottage's back bedroom. I had brought serious doubts about our relationship to that room. Something was missing. I could spend weeks away from her and not miss her company. I knew our relationship was over, but I could not quite believe it or admit it to myself.

The Spirit knew. He would have told me sooner had I listened. What I needed more than a wife was a family. And that was what I had begun to realize as I became involved among the churches in Detroit. Had Eleanor and I married, we might have experienced family, living among the Christians in Detroit, but it would not have been the same.

Hazel was a daughter in the family. I married into a family of believers who knew Hazel and whose children had been taught by her in Sunday school. They were a family among whom we could grow, raise our children, exercise our gifts. It probably wouldn't have been quite the same with Eleanor. Only the Spirit knew, and I finally listened.

Sometime along the way I had told Hazel about Eleanor, and later we had the opportunity to extend hospitality to Eleanor and her companion several years into our marriage. She had decided to follow up on an earlier interest to minister among native Americans, so she and her partner had come to Detroit to share their work and raise funds. Hazel suggested that they stay with us overnight. In church the following day, they shared their vision for their work and then were off to their next assignment.

13

Eye-Opening Conversations

THE INVITATION CAME FROM LeRoy Bechler. He was one of the leaders of a small settlement of Mennonite believers who had settled in Saginaw, Michigan, to minister in the black communities there. I scarcely knew where Saginaw was, let alone that Mennonites were active there. I knew that Mennonites were not Amish and that they did not all live on farms, but I had not met any in active ministry in the cities where I had worked. Saginaw was a typical working-class city in Michigan whose fortunes were tied to the auto industry. It was divided along economic and class lines, the black community segregated in the genteel manner that northern whites dictated.

The year was 1958, and in the ensuing years it would be my privilege to serve with similar Mennonite leaders in black communities from Saginaw to St. Ann to St. Louis, from Chicago's west side to Los Angeles's Watts and Inglewood. They would eventually put a new face on the Mennonite Church in America and unite rural congregations in sustained ministries to reach urban people with the gospel and its call to wage peace instead of war.

It was this later emphasis that occasioned Bechler's call. Black people in urban centers had never heard of Mennonites, and yet here were these very nice people, loving and helpful. Caring for our young people, opening their doors of worship to the community, behaving as if they really loved black people. "Pannell, would you come up and preach for us, and demonstrate that we are believers as you are?"

That first weekend trip was followed by other trips to that city. It opened the door for me to minister in congregations of Mennonites in small towns and rural communities across the Midwest, most of whom rarely saw a person of color.

Vernon Miller was a Mennonite pastor in Cleveland, Ohio. He and his wife, Helen, had settled and worked in black communities in the city and in Shaker Heights, a suburb where black middle-class citizens had begun to move. He founded what they called Lee Heights Community Church, with "Mennonite" in small print. Vernon was concerned about community development, and was committed to his own intellectual growth. He continued to study and eventually earned a master's degree. Whenever I preached in the congregation, I lived with Vern and his family, and our conversations were lively and entertaining. Helen even laughed at my jokes.

My political education began with Vern. The occasion was the debate in Washington over whether an American spy plane had been shot down over Russia. President Eisenhower vehemently denied that such a thing had happened. I tended to agree with Ike. I had voted for him; I trusted him. Besides, he was an American, and Americans don't spy on other people. Not at 40,000 feet at least.

Vern laughed his gentle Mennonite laugh and challenged my naivete. "You really think Americans are above such behavior?" he asked. He began to challenge my marriage of evangelical faith and patriotism. It was a soft assault on my theology and an introduction to the Anabaptist worldview. Before the week was over, the Russians displayed the U-2 plane that was shot down, and Francis Gary Powers, the American pilot who was flying it.

Of all the Mennonite pastors and leaders in many places, Vern Miller served me at the deepest levels. He gave me a new set of ears with which to hear what my evangelical associates were beginning to say about the civil rights movement and set in motion a lifelong critique of so-called Christian nationalism. His parting gift to me was a copy of M. L. King's early book *The Strength to Love*, in which King's sermons articulate a social gospel.

Vern was the intellectual among the Mennonite leaders I worked with. He understood the importance of the city from a kingdom perspective. The other pastors would gradually move in that direction, but Vern knew that it was in the cities where the witness of peace would be finally settled.

At the opposite end of that leadership spectrum was Fred Augsburger. Along with his wife and children, Fred had moved into the black community on the west side of Youngstown, Ohio. I was invited to preach a series there in the fall of 1966. I liked everything about the setting, especially its parklike foliage and lovely golf course. The congregation was mostly black, with attending white Mennonites who assisted in the development of the congregation.

All was going well until Fred approached me to ask if I would be willing to take off my wedding ring. He let me know that jewelry was forbidden among the Mennonites there. I told him that I would take off my socks if it would help, and we laughed our way to an understanding. I took off the ring. I also told Fred that I really didn't think that they wanted to lead our people down that old path.

We parted after the series, and I received an invitation to return the following year. I did so. And not only was there no request to take the ring off, but there were new hymnals also. It seems that Fred's father had told him that they should use a hymnal that was more congenial to the congregation's traditions. "Besides," he claimed, "that old black volume we use is killing us Mennonites."

I decided to expose Fred to golf. He was awkward, to say the least, but understood his need to broaden his exposure to city life. The following year I returned, and he had purchased a set of clubs. Unfortunately, he had opted for a set that he could afford, and the store had sold him wooden shafted clubs. They looked as if they had come over on the Mayflower. We went to the course, and they didn't last beyond the first five holes. I thought we would die laughing.

The meetings went well. I learned that one of the members, a white man, was going to Scottsdale, Pennsylvania, on business. I had wanted to visit that place since I had learned that it was the denomination's center of publications. He agreed to take me along, and it was there that I met the young man who was in charge of Mennonite Youth Fellowship. Gene Herr welcomed me to his office, and we began a discussion about how to transform the broad network of Mennonite young people who were involved in MYF.

We clicked, and he called his wife, Mary, to ask if he could bring a guest for lunch. She was a young mother and a very welcoming hostess. Indeed, our wives were the same age, and we were raising families of the same ages also. Their oldest son was named Philip. So also was ours. That meeting was to be the first of many as we worked together to effect change among young people.

I participated in national conferences in exotic places such as Oregon and the Kishacoquillas Valley of Pennsylvania. In Oregon I listened to the voice of its governor, Mark Hatfield, and thought he was the best speaker of the lot.

It was in Gene's company that I was introduced to the early network of Presbyterian leaders whose full-blown vision became Faith at Work. Years later Gene and I would travel with the Faith at Work team in a series of clergy conferences that stretched from Atlanta and Dallas to Los Angeles, Chicago, and New York City.

At a Faith at Work gathering in New York City, I met Clarence Jordan. His lectures with a few of us in a farmhouse on Long Island changed the course of several lives. He spoke about Jesus and discipleship. Jordan was becoming known in the North because of his work directing Koinonia Farm in Americus, Georgia. Koinonia was not just a farm but also a gathering of people with mixed ethnic backgrounds and physical needs. Jordan and his cohorts were well known in the South for their communal lifestyle and commitment to justice. This brought them into conflict with local white citizen groups and leading Southern Baptist churches.

Jordan's nephew was also well known in the state because of his work with Jimmy Carter. In the ensuing years, my relationship with the Mennonite movement became among the richest of my career. I would be invited to preach in congregations from Ohio to Kansas and was asked to speak at spiritual emphasis sessions in their colleges from Eastern Mennonite in Virginia to Hesston College in Kansas. I would work with Myron Augsburger, one of the most effective evangelistic preachers of our day. I led the singing and handled some of the social engagements of meetings in Miami. I had conversations with him in his successful radio chat sessions.

It was in the office of John Howard Yoder, the theological voice of that movement and of a growing number of younger Americans, where I first learned that not all Mennonites considered themselves evangelicals. I was preaching in a Mennonite congregation near Goshen, Indiana, and asked to chat with Yoder. He was generous with his time. I sought his advice about the upcoming gathering of evangelicals in Berlin. I had been invited to be a delegate and wondered what that could mean. He startled me by saying that he knew nothing about it, and during the ensuing conversation I became aware that he did not think of himself as a card-carrying evangelical.

It was one in a series of eye-opening conversations I was to have with this remarkable man. I did not find him to be a person with whom I would enjoy a night on the town. His social skills left much to be desired. One would have only to read his writings, especially his pathbreaking *The Politics of Jesus*, to know how significant he was to the church's understanding of God's kingdom order. Imagine how his ideas about the politics of Jesus would sit with a devotee of Plymouth Brethren thought. Or a gathering of Billy Graham-generation evangelicals.

In that same year I received an invitation to speak in chapel at Wheaton College. Located thirty miles west of Chicago in the town of Wheaton, the evangelical college was made famous by alumnus Billy Graham.

I have little recollection of how that invitation came about, but I suspect it had something to do with my involvement with InterVarsity in Detroit. I chose to address the issue of color by discussing what one black scholar had called "negritude." Of course, I made sure that the outline was suitably alliterative and sufficiently supported by Scripture.

The presentation apparently went well. Lamberta Voget, a member of the faculty, contacted Joe Bayly, then the editor of *His* magazine, the flagship journal of InterVarsity Christian Fellowship. His follow up with me resulted in a warm friendship that lasted for years.

It was Joe who introduced me to the great preacher from Harlem, Gardner Taylor. Said Joe, "If Taylor preached anywhere near Chicago, I would join his church tomorrow just to hear him preach." Joe was my only connection with InterVarsity until several years later, when C. Stacey Woods showed up at our Assembly for our annual Bible conference. He knew Mr. Nottage through their shared Brethren roots.

14

"Who Are You Guys?"

"We're going to change it," he said. "We're going to take it over and change it and we want you to be part of it." The "it" was the national office of Youth for Christ.

From its earliest days as the platform of a young Billy Graham and a small army of young, aggressive local leaders, the organization had grown to become an international presence in youth ministries. Paul Robbins and I were talking in his office in Fort Wayne, Indiana. We had both graduated from the same Bible college. I trusted Paul. We were friends, but I responded that the Youth for Christ I knew in Detroit was lily white and segregated. He replied, "Maybe so. I don't doubt it, but we're going to change it."

What a new generation of leadership had in mind was establishing a strong central office in Wheaton. Youth for Christ didn't function as an organization with a strong central office. It functioned as a name with hundreds of event-oriented ministries scattered in key cities across America. Each of these local ministries was developed as an autonomous center, free to design its own strategies for engaging the world of young people. The role of the central office was merely a figurehead function. The real power and responsibility for the image of Youth for Christ was in the hands of key leaders in key cities in the country. They were outstanding leaders, all of them white. The trick would be to wrest this individualism from these men and centralize at a strong center. They wanted to make it something like Young Life, which would allow them to develop a stronger financial base and strengthen the overseas network.

The young Jay Kesler, the veteran Sam Wolgemuth, Paul Robbins, and their families moved to Wheaton to begin the takeover. It took several years, but I joined these men. I was to leave the organization two times over the next years, once as a member of the leadership team, and the other as chairman of the board.

"The takeover didn't work," Paul confessed to me. He too had left, in his case to become the vice-president of *Christianity Today* magazine. It didn't work because the guys in the field would not surrender autonomy. It also failed because the same guys could not take on the challenge of a changing urban landscape. They followed their constituents to the suburbs. Neither they nor Young Life could face into the challenge posed by millions of young people whose complexion was unlike their own. It became clear to me that there was no place left for me at the headquarters.

I did become attracted to the leadership and strategies of the program in Chicago. It was integrated under the leadership of Jack Daniel, who didn't allow his whiteness to get in the way of listening to the black leadership he had recruited. My attraction was shared, and Jack finally proposed that I leave headquarters and join his staff.

After some serious wrestling, Hazel and I agreed to move to Chicago. The "for sale" sign was in the front yard, and we began to look for housing on Chicago's South Side. It was in the fall of 1966. Watts had exploded in Los Angeles, and Detroit followed with its urban revolt soon after. I knew America's black communities had turned a corner in their relations with white America. I suspected this would also be true of relations between those same communities and white-led Christian organizations. The sign in the front yard was removed.

I received a letter from Carl Henry, and that in itself was noteworthy. He invited me to participate in an international gathering of evangelicals at the World Congress on Evangelism that was to meet in Berlin, West Germany, in 1966. He wanted me to prepare a paper for the gathering that would be shared with delegates and would become a part of the conversations about evangelism. I was greatly pleased, and flattered. It had become clear to me in reading about this gathering that it was an enormous undertaking, and to become a delegate would be quite an honor.

I was to learn from this experience how deep and wide the connections ran between the evangelical network across the world. It was unprecedented in scope. I had never seen such a representation of the Christian movement worldwide. When His Majesty Haile Selassie of Ethiopia walked down the center aisle to his place on the platform, I knew this was more than a gathering. It had become a spectacle. As Oral Roberts put it on one of his appearances, "Only Billy Graham could have pulled this off."

By the second day, I had begun to realize that the American delegates seemed to have a different spirit about them. Delegates from the Third World seemed to have come with more energy, more excitement bordering on expectation. Or maybe just gratitude. The Americans seemed to be more blasé. They were the heads of leading evangelistic organizations and mission groups. They were presidents of Christian colleges and seminaries. They acted as if they belonged. I felt that I had already met these leaders. They were mostly white and male. I had caddied for them at the country club.

The paper I prepared sought to highlight the challenge of evangelism in a world that was becoming urban. It caught the attention of a reporter from the *Detroit Free Press*. Unfortunately, he (or his editor) gave it a spin I had not intended. When it appeared in the paper back home it read like I had engaged in a debate with Mr. Graham on the issues I highlighted. Hazel was impressed but was made uncomfortable when a piece of hate mail arrived at our house. The letter's author suggested that the city should turn one of its downtown buildings into a crematorium for the likes of people like her husband.

While still in Berlin, I had been pleased to receive an invitation from Hudson Armerding, the president of Wheaton College. He suggested that we have lunch together. I thought that this was timely, since my next assignment upon returning to the States was to be the speaker at Wheaton's annual Spiritual Emphasis Week. I told the president how pleased I was to have been invited and mentioned that I had received letters from several students expressing high expectations for the series. They pledged their prayers toward this end. Armerding was grateful that such exchanges had been made but didn't seem to be altogether satisfied. I wouldn't learn why until after the first chapel service.

I preached about God's love and our call to discipleship in a world in dire need of tough love. The response seemed to be favorable, especially among some of the guys who, I had observed, were listening from their front row seats. They waited for me after chapel. We quickly found ourselves in a lively discussion about what I had said. They were pleased.

Dr. Armerding was not. He motioned for me to join him. "That's what I was trying to tell you in Berlin," he said. To this day I have no idea what he had said in Berlin that had carried over to Wheaton. He was upset because I challenged his white student body to choose between a cozy life in the suburbs or a radical commitment to a broken society in our cities. "So you were setting me up in Berlin, right?" I asked. He admitted that he was, but not in the way it sounded. "Why didn't you just come right out and tell me what was really on your mind?" I asked.

Our conversation ended, and I returned to the students who had waited for us to finish. The first comment was, "Well, he got to you, didn't he?" They knew him. If the students thought that they knew him, I wondered if he knew them.

Armerding was from the Plymouth Brethren tradition and so was I. But he was a retired naval officer, so of course he was deeply committed to order, rules, and regulations, as well as orthodoxy. That commitment may also account for his upset at my question later that week: "Why is it easier for a major Christian university to support the presence of an ROTC unit than to establish a center for the study of nonviolence?"

On another visit to the school, I mingled with students, and after one gathering a young woman said, "I read your book, and I expected an angrier man today. You don't seem to be the same person who wrote that book." She sounded confused and perhaps a bit disappointed. "Well," I said, "I have to ask myself if coming to places like this is worth coming again. I am coming here for you—for students. You are why I come."

President Armerding was listening to this conversation. We were not enemies, but we were from different sides of town.

In retrospect I think I would have been helped greatly had I known about the history of Wheaton College. So also would the black students who had been newly recruited by the school from places like Chicago. I knew more of the history of the place than they did, but I had no idea of its long-standing position as one of several key bastions of fundamentalism and missionary involvement. This is a most impressive history.

But although Wheaton's founder, Jonathan Blanchard, was an abolitionist, the college had long since walked away from its foundation. It was now white culture. Taking some of its cues from the ministry of Dwight L. Moody and the Moody Bible Institute, the college followed white evangelicalism from city to suburbs. The fundamentalism and revivalism it championed and promoted never quite accommodated itself to the urban America that was emerging after World War II. If one were to inject the issue of race into this mix, it would further cloud the attempts of the school to reach out to young people of color. Were they offering us a first-class education, or were they trying to save us from our cultural entrapment?

The summer months in the 1960s were replete with conferences scattered across the country that brought together the cream of evangelical celebrities in music, preaching, and Bible studies. In many ways these conferences kept alive the fundamentalist-evangelical network across the nation. I attended these conferences in the tri-state area of Illinois, Michigan, and Indiana.

Winona Lake in northern Indiana stood at the center of it all. Its Bible conferences played an integral role in the rise of fundamentalism in the twentieth century. Audiences gathered to hear well-known Christian personalities and Bible teachers speak on popular theological currents, missionary themes, end-times speculation, and renewal.

One of the featured speakers at the annual Youth for Christ bash at Winona Lake was Tom Skinner. Born and raised in Harlem, Skinner's reputation was on the rise as he shared his remarkable story of being converted from gang activities in Harlem. Prior to Winona Lake, Tom had a highly successful evangelistic ministry in the Caribbean. He was the featured speaker on nearly twenty radio stations stretching from Philadelphia to Okinawa.

Several years prior, the Christian Assemblies of Detroit determined to hold an evangelistic week to reach out to the central city's black community. I was part of that network. It was decided that we would invite a young preacher from New York who seemed to have an effective ministry among similar congregations in the East and in the Caribbean. We asked for the use of a large auditorium in the area, and Louis Johnson, pastor of Friendship Baptist Church, was pleased to lease their sanctuary to us. We invited Tom Skinner to be our preacher. I was to lead the singing and handle the platform.

The series began on a Sunday evening. Tom arrived on Monday and never gave a reason for his absence. I was stuck with preaching the opening sermon after dragging out the music in the hope that he would arrive. The rest of the week went along in normal fashion, and our relationship was amicable if not overly cordial. His demeanor was distant, his preaching quite impressive. That is, until somewhere in the middle of the week, when I began to recognize his sermons. I would return home in the evenings and take down my copy of Major Ian Thomas's *The Saving Life of Christ*, a work on the deeper Christian life. In those pages I could read the next night's sermon, almost word for word. We called it plagiarism in polite circles, but when I called Skinner on it, he shrugged it off as simply passing on a common legacy of biblical truth. After all, he replied, "all truth is God's truth."

Years later when I worked with Mr. Thomas, I recited this incident without any names. He basically said the same thing as Tom had. Skinner preached Thomas's stuff far better than Thomas.

The Detroit series ended, and Tom went on his way. We did not see each other until the meeting at Winona Lake. But much had changed in the culture, and we both knew it was an opportune time for us to pool our resources.

Tom had received an invitation to conduct a citywide evangelistic series in Newark, New Jersey. The city had been shaken to its core by what the Kerner Commission Report called "unrest." It was far worse than that. When I arrived the following year, the place still smelled of smoke and unrest. Had it been an Irish neighborhood, I thought, they would have burned the place long ago.

I was impressed by Tom's invitation and took the possibilities back to Detroit. Hazel listened carefully. She would be the one to ask about the financial arrangements, and I told her that I did not know for certain but thought it was worth pursuing. She agreed, and it was arranged for me to fly to New York for a meeting with Skinner and his board chairman Frank Pickell. Hazel was pleased that I was pleased. She was also satisfied with the salary the organization offered me, the first salary of my ministry life.

But things were not always easy. Sandwiched between two movements, King's and Graham's, we were black evangelists in a tradition of urban evangelism and yet not a part of a fundamentalism or evangelicalism that gave such ministries its birth. Small wonder we would be asked, as the work developed, "Who are you guys?" Local leaders were attracted by our work but put off by the format. Or they were confused by their association of the messages with our obvious blackness.

I had expected we would be the main attraction when we arrived in Newark in 1968. I was wrong. The city had been the location of a historic gathering of black intellectuals and clergymen the previous year. It was dubbed the Black Power Conference and was a continuation of major discussions among these leaders. It was black power over against the more moderate offerings of M. L. King Jr. One could hear the clash in the verbal dueling of Stokely Carmichael and King. It was this clash between black power and nonviolence that set the agenda for black theologians such as

James Cone. He made theological history with the release of his book *Black Theology and Black Power*, in which he asserted that "Black Power is Christ's central message to twentieth-century America."

But the book that had caught my attention was written by a black clergyman. Dr. Nathan Wright, an Episcopal minister, had set his sights on the challenge of black Americans who had become the center of America's largest cities. His book *Black Power and Urban Unrest* was a different kind of response to the Kerner Report. Wright had chaired the first National Conference on Black Power in Newark in July 1967. A secretary from his office gave me a copy of the concluding statements of that gathering.

The document was news to me. As I read it, I knew that it represented new challenges for any evangelical who wanted to know what the salient features were in the battle for the soul of America. And the militants who gave birth to this trinity of expectations—identity, community, and power—argued that anyone with any hope of relating to the black community had to affirm these values and contribute to their realization. It was from that document that I realized we had to incorporate these values into our ministry. These would be the same issues any culture would need to address if it were to fulfill its own deep promises. The universality of these issues made it certain that the proponents of black theology could get an audience in South Africa and South America. Indeed, wherever oppression could be tied to the abuse of power.

But other evangelicals besides Skinner Crusades were drawn to Newark in the late fall of 1968 and into the next year. Campus Crusade was there, as was InterVarsity, and later came students from Philadelphia's Conwell Theological Seminary led by Stewart Barton Babbage.

We had conversations with most of the representatives of these groups, and it was my task to coordinate some of it. I discovered that the group from Philadelphia suited my understanding of urban inquisitiveness. By their questions you shall know them. Representatives of Campus Crusade were least inclined to ask questions. They had brought their answers with them.

Newark became a learning experience for us. Tom and I were not strangers to evangelistic work, and we thought that we knew something about the gospel. As a product of an evangelical Bible college, I would have been greatly helped if our educators had informed us of the changes that were taking place in the world into which they were sending us with the gospel. But I had graduated a bit too early for that, I guess. Yet strange new energies had been released in the body politic in the late forties, early fifties. A world war had ended, and the country was reaffirming its commitment, not to matters of justice for which wars were fought, but to the good life. GIs needed education and new housing, and the American taste for travel and new cars had to be satisfied. America was indeed the land of the free, the home of the brave, but it was also the land blessed with a birthright to prosper. The business of America was business.

But prosperity was not to be extended to all Americans, including those who had fought to keep it free. As it became more and more intolerable for black Americans to be denied access to the corridors of achievement, the cities exploded in protest.

Our series in Newark came on the heels of the admission by the Kerner Report, the national advisory commission on civil disorder, that "the country was moving toward two societies, one black, one white, separate and unequal," and that "white society is deeply implicated in the ghetto. White institutions created it, white institutions maintain it and white society condones it." Given this reality, it should have come as no surprise that black leaders, ecclesiastical and secular, would demand something beyond the strength to love. The issue was not love, but power.

15

Pulled Between Two Understandings of the Gospel

Taylor Branch, in the preface to his history of the civil rights era, *Parting the Waters: America in the King Years, 1954–63*, posits that Martin Luther King Jr.'s life "is the best and most important metaphor for American history in the watershed postwar years." Yet another thesis would be that Billy Graham's life and ministry is the most important metaphor for evangelical history during the same period. This thesis is mine.

Billy Graham was white evangelicalism. He was also white America; he represented the kind of Christian life that white America preferred, consistent with all the other trappings associated with the American way. He was an evangelist. White people could accept that, even those who were not interested in becoming his kind of Christian. They did not want a prophet, certainly not a black prophet. But most Americans were comfortable with what they saw in the handsome preacher. His Jesus made a good American, a warmhearted neighbor comfortable with the aspirations of a land of the free and home of the brave.

Two men—both Southerners, both Americans, both preachers—one black and the other white. Both deeply committed to calling America back to God, back to the fulfillment of the dream expressed in the nation's sacred literature. They were friendly with one another, though perhaps not friends, respectful of each other's calling, the one content to be called an evangelist, the other wanting to be a drum major for Jesus.

Skinner and I, without giving it much thought, would spend our brief career together sandwiched between these two theses, pulled between two understandings of the gospel of Christ, two models of how discipleship behaved in a world gone urban.

Evangelicals would take on the task of calling America to repent and turn back to God. This part of the society, largely white in its evangelical makeup, would release an enormous energy to ensure that America became Christian. Revivalism was the means by which this was to be attained, and the vessels through which it was to flow were a generation of men and women, mostly white men who had experienced the second world war, many through military service. This explosion of revivalism gave birth to fervent evangelistic strategies that stretched from the Midwest to Korea, the Far East, and South America.

I had become familiar with most of the names associated with this movement as I was completing Bible college in the early fifties and into the early sixties. I learned to hide my pocketbook when Bob Pierce took the offering at a Winona Lake gathering. He had left the directorship of a Youth for Christ program to found World Vision International.

The largest boost to this movement took place in Los Angeles with the evangelistic crusade led by Billy Graham. His pitch was aimed at bringing revival to America, and for the rest of his life that was his main focus. And he looked the part; handsome, white, impeccably dressed in both apparel and culture. His team was what revival looked and sounded like. Revivalism was in the air. It was felt in hundreds of Youth for Christ rallies across the nation and the world. Thousands of prayer meetings had sprung up across the land, and a new generation of preachers began to mount pulpits on street corners and in cathedrals, calling America back to God.

Radio assumed a prominent place in this revival. Among the most recognized voices heard on networks across the land was that of Charles E. Fuller, along with his wife, Grace, whom he affectionately called "honey" as she read the letters that had been sent to the ministry. There really was a hunger in the land for something more than the good life as defined by General Motors or Dinah Shore. This movement became so powerful that *Time* magazine dubbed 1976 "The Year of the Evangelical."

"Revival" and "evangelical" became synonymous in both the Christian and the secular mind. Mr. Graham was playing golf and dining among the movers and shakers in American political and social life.

But another revival movement had taken shape in the land, and it was black. Called the civil rights movement, it also concerned itself with bringing America back to God and to the promise held out to all Americans in the Constitution. But its main themes were justice and reconciliation, and if its centerpiece was not the cross as Mr. Graham preached it—well, black people knew more about that than did their white counterparts. Black people had been asking about the cross for many years; it was the motif in a popular hymn inquiring who had been there. Newark became, for us, another center in the struggle for the soul of America. The soul of the country had moved from the wheat and cornfields of Iowa to the cities. America had become an urban society, and white believers, those who truly hoped for a revival, had begun to abandon these cities for the comfort and safety of the suburbs. These were the elements of "revival" in America with which we had to deal when we arrived in Newark: the hopes and fears of white evangelicals and the hopes and fears of black people, including Christians, who were still chafing under the revolts in the streets. Christians, including black evangelicals, would choose the power of the Holy Spirit over any other claimant using the term.

So, we would preach to audiences composed of black and white Christians whose hopes and fears were tied to the agenda of Jesus Christ. But black believers knew that their white brothers and sisters had more than Jesus going for them. Dominick Spina, director of police in Newark, knew that too, as did the Jewish leaders with whom he had developed a cozy relationship. It would become clear as we moved into the series that there was a larger issue to be addressed than simply calling people to believe in Jesus as Savior. We had some growing up to do.

Tom Skinner came to Newark on the heels of impressive success as an evangelist in the Caribbean. These events were sponsored by local Plymouth Brethren congregations and lay leaders. He was accompanied on several of these meetings by his wife, Vivian, who was a gifted musician. Friends from his highly successful crusade in Harlem accompanied him as part of his prayer entourage.

Skinner was busy speaking all over the place, especially at the invitation of white groups. My impression was that there was a strong hope among these evangelicals that a crusade led by a black team could go a long way toward saving the city from "them." Nothing ever got said in that way, but the hope was in the air. But there was a growing tension between what

Skinner was preaching in the auditorium and what he was preaching in the suburban churches.

In the one place he could remind our audience of a black Billy Graham, but as the series moved on he began to sound more like the ex-urban gang leader turned Christian. By the time the series ended in Newark, Skinner was becoming the great white hope among everyone from local Christians to the likes of Jack Wyrtzen and other leading evangelicals along the eastern coast. Skinner knew Wyrtzen, having had a successful ministry at his camp for young people.

Wyrtzen had a large influence among white evangelicals in the East. He had been an early protégé of Percy Crawford, an evangelist whose creative leadership would result in the founding of King's College in 1938. These men promoted rallies that put thousands of young people into such venues as Madison Square Garden and Carnegie Hall during an earlier decade of evangelistic activity. They believed that if America was to be saved it would be through its young people, and revival was the means by which this transformation would happen.

But as our involvement in Newark increased, and as Skinner's influence widened, there was some concern that Tom was in danger of straying from the "simple gospel." Here again one could feel the power of the civil rights movement as this influence continued to offer the country an alternative to the preaching of the gospel by white evangelists. We were caught squarely in the middle of these clashing ideologies.

An example of this growing concern occurred over lunch after the crusade. We had met to discuss an offer by some highly placed members of the art culture to conduct an outdoor meeting in Newark. Jerome Hines, of the Metropolitan Opera, had offered his influence and presence to headline such an event. Skinner was up for it. Wyrtzen was against it and voiced his concern over the inclusion of Hines especially. His objection centered on Hines's use of a four-letter word in the lyrics of a pop opera song.

It was clear that the real issues around that luncheon table had to do with power and influence. Who would have the ear of Skinner as he moved into the future. Whose ministry would benefit from such influence. Who would eventually claim responsibility for having influenced the career of this fast-rising black evangelist. We were to learn that this was a key issue as our influence grew over the next several years.

Finally, one leading evangelical took us aside and admitted, "There are people out there who want you guys to succeed. But not too much. So behave; keep your noses clean." Wyrtzen and I had skirmished at lunch over a matter having to do with Wheaton College. I challenged his take on the issue, and he was visibly upset. I was not prepared for Newark's deep divisions along ethnic and economic lines.

After that lunch, Wyrtzen called our chairman demanding that Skinner fire me. "He'll ruin Tom," he explained. The chairman was unmoved. Blacks and whites vied for leadership as they sought to put the city back together again. A cross-section of the evangelical faith community, black and white, saw that we were part of the answer. If anybody could put Humpty Dumpty together again, it was Jesus.

Tom had had enormous success in evangelistic crusades from Harlem to Guyana and other points throughout the Caribbean. He had heralded these meetings in his well-received book *Black and Free*, released in 1968.

I had begun reading material dealing with America's urban crisis, and the growing literature grappling with theologies of power, psychology, and urban life. I passed some of this on to Tom when we huddled before evening meetings. Several years later I would introduce him to the thinking of that splendid prophet from Georgia, Clarence Jordan. Tom was a sponge, possessed of a quick mind and a remarkable ability to take ideas from different sources, blend them, or appropriate them in a sermon—often that same evening. He was busy, so I fed him what I was reading.

Skinner was preaching in and around Newark, but he was more at home there than I was. After all, Newark is but a long shot across the bridge from Harlem. But it was New Jersey, a remarkable study in cultures by itself. We met Jews and police officers, including those who were assigned to guard us during our services at the Newark Coliseum. We had received death threats. We were evangelists, and we thought we knew how to call men and women to faith in Jesus Christ, but we were black men also. I recall the woman who approached me in one evening gathering to tell me that she was confused. "You seem to be such a nice young man," she said, but "how could you have written that awful book?" The book was *My Friend, the Enemy*, published in 1968.

Her question was intriguing and amusing, but what it revealed was that I was not fully aware at that time that the evangelical church was not simply out to lunch socially and politically; it was also estranged from this kind of thinking.

When my son learned, many years after Newark, that I was contemplating writing a memoir, I asked him what would interest him about his father if I were to write such a book. He replied, "I'd like to know how you changed."

By then he was out of college and had morphed into a fine clinical psychologist. He was only eleven years old when the woman posed the question, but she was asking a related question, only hers was more of an accusation: "How dare you change?"

16

My Love Affair with Books

I AM NOT CERTAIN about the timing of it, but somewhere after Bible college I realized that I liked ideas. In preaching I enjoyed the interplay of ideas and words. I liked sermon preparation, the challenge of reading both the text of Scripture and whatever helps I needed to illumine the passage.

But I gradually realized that there was a world out there about which I was largely ignorant. There were other issues to contend with, deep stirrings in society that I was ill prepared to examine—Korea, Vietnam, and the ongoing influence of the civil rights movement, for example. Most Christian bookstores didn't carry literature that examined these issues. Neither did the usual offerings of the newspapers in communities where I worked.

I needed help, and to my surprise it came as I began to travel by air. The ideas that were stimulating, that challenged my evangelistic mindset, came about courtesy of American, Northwest, and United Airlines. I discovered a wealth of ideas in these magazine racks, and I began to arrive early so as to be at the head of the line to get to the magazine rack. Here I read about current affairs and the world of ideas contained in editorials and articles in the *Saturday Review of Literature*, *Esquire*, *Life*, and *Look*.

I gradually gave myself permission to be what some people had been accusing me of being: an intellectual. It was a nasty word among many Christians, including most of the preachers with whom I worked. After all, preaching, if it was to be biblical, ought to be simple. That is, the preacher's task was to preach the simple gospel.

Years later I engaged in conversation with a member of Billy Graham's team. I was working with Tom Skinner at the time. He took the occasion to encourage us to preach the simple gospel, "like Billy does." I asked him what he considered to be "simple" about the gospel. The conversation ended there. Could he have been using code words to express that the simple gospel that Billy preached was what black Americans really needed? Not civil rights or justice or equal access to quality education?

I had begun to change my thinking about a lot of things before Newark. Some of it had to do with the civil rights movement and the place that critical thinking had in the life and ministry of young M. L. King Jr. He was far more sophisticated than any evangelical preacher I knew. To be sure, his was a more liberal cultural and theological orientation than the term "evangelical" could comfortably encompass. But he was a preacher, a Baptist preacher at that. And his hero, his model of love and justice, was Jesus.

The cultural, political, and theological orientation I had imbibed as a young preacher was reflective of early fundamentalism and revivalism. The goal, if society was to be changed, was to get people converted, born again. The prayer was to persuade God to heal the land by getting people to repent of their sins and turn from their wicked ways.

But what if the country was already Christian, for the most part at least, especially the part of the society that was white? Well, they at least could support evangelistic efforts to reach those who were not Christians, even those people of color within our own borders, our cities, etc. Mr. Graham could reach the white populations in and around our major cities; Skinner and Pannell could spearhead evangelistic thrusts among non-white people at the core of those cities. But evangelical thinking was that the answer to human need was the simple gospel and revival.

Another challenge gnawing at my mind was posed by the tradition of holiness or spirituality. I encountered this line of thought in Bible college but didn't understand that its roots were in early fundamentalism or the many other schools of deeper life revivalism. I knew about how these old movements sounded and behaved because I had been part of them, had tried to partake of the experiences prescribed. I went to the conferences, and most of my colleagues in evangelism were part of these movements. We were all basically anti-intellectual, not meaning that we could not think but that our thinking was slanted or confined within the parameters of what worked. And what was supposed to work was revival. Without knowing it, we had become doers, evangelistic workers; we were talented and creative, and we did strive to be spiritual. But what did spirituality, of whatever tradition, have to do with the movements taking place on the streets of our major cities? What was the possible connection of spirituality and the Black Panthers in Oakland? Or that growing cloud of witnesses who walked urban streets protesting the war in Vietnam?

17

"The Liberator Has Come!"

Carl Ellis was an evangelical student at Hampton Institute. He was from northern Indiana, raised by a godly mother, and influenced as a lad by the radio ministry of the Moody Bible Institute. He, along with other Christians at Hampton, had heard of Skinner and invited Tom and me to the campus for a week of meetings. The campus was alive with the creative agitation that one finds when upheavals in society wash up on academic shores. It was a time for long hair and dashikis. The personalities of the day were Dr. King, Malcolm X, and Stokely Carmichael, and there were black students who wondered what Jesus had to say about "the revolution." Or "Did Billy Graham send you guys?" We preached Jesus Christ to them, assuring them that Jesus had his own revolution and that they were invited to join it.

The week went well but raised the question among some about the desirability of forming a campus ministry under the Skinner umbrella. The ministries of InterVarsity and Campus Crusade were judged as being too white. Black students were celebrating blackness. Along with Ellis, Tom and I drafted a proposal that would establish a campus ministry under the Skinner banner. We took the idea to the board and the work became official. I was selected to direct the new venture.

The brains behind the work belonged to Ellis. Carl was an American theologian and culture guru who worried that American culture was falling away from God. He and I would spend hours together in his room thinking about culture wars and plotting strategies about evangelism on black campuses. We followed the black students we knew on campuses in the Southeast, beginning at Hampton.

We learned of Carl's attraction to the cultural critiques of Francis Schaeffer. The little man with the Swiss leggings had captured a large swath of college students from his L'Abri center in Switzerland. We decided to send Carl to study with Shaeffer. It was money well spent, as Carl was the theologian of our team.

The campus ministry was centered on black campuses in the East and South. Carl knew students in most of these places. The problem was that we didn't have sufficient personnel to serve these campuses. Tom had a busy schedule as his popularity among white evangelical ministries increased, and I was occupied with work among Christian colleges. It was decided that we should focus our energies on major events in the evangelical calendar.

That led us to concentrate on the upcoming Urbana conference for collegians sponsored by InterVarsity Christian Fellowship. Since 1947, meeting every three years, Urbana was the flagship event sponsored by IV. It drew thousands of young people from around the world and featured leading missiologists, missionaries, and Bible teachers.

Indeed, the focus was on overseas missions. This was one of the reasons this ministry did not attract black students. Another reason was that IV didn't follow up and maintain the connections it had with key black evangelicals who were already within its orbit. These men were all card-carrying evangelicals. Most of them had been educated in evangelical schools, men like Ron Potter, Benn Johnson, and Elward Ellis. Paul Gibson was a Harvard grad headed for a career in medicine. So what was the problem?

I came to understand that a key issue was the fear within IV's mission leadership that relationships with black leaders might influence IV to embrace more liberal social and political agendas, as had occurred earlier in the Student Volunteer Movement. InterVarsity was convinced that social action interests had killed the Student Volunteer Movement. This fear was reinforced among evangelicals by the impact of the civil rights movement in the country. Black evangelicals were stuck between our loyalties to our evangelical networks and our loyalty to and deep appreciation of the work of Dr. King and the movement.

Black students were asking: what about social action? How does one preach the gospel as if people were not social creatures, as if their lives were not impacted by social and political issues? Besides all this, black students knew that the world had turned urban, and that a typical Urbana platform scarcely reflected this reality.

Prominent Bible expositors, such as John Stott from London, offered very little for non-white students whose mission field was often just down the block. The leadership of IV, though sensitive to all these issues, was hesitant to move forward.

So black student leaders held an all-night prayer meeting. Convinced that God was not a white racist, they offered themselves to God for his work alongside InterVarsity leaders. Ellis, along with key black students, entered into further negotiations with IV leadership. It was decided that black students needed to be better informed about Urbana. It was further decided that a film should be developed with black leadership depicting the importance of the event. Ellis would write the script. The film would also invite black students to participate in the total event as contributors to the broader agenda of the historic movement of missions to all the world.

The decision was made to invite key leaders among an emergent black evangelical network to be present to give leadership to the event. The event would spotlight the ministry of Tom Skinner as a keynote speaker.

Urbana 1970 was a turning point in the history of that event. An unprecedented turnout of black students participated, especially in special sessions dealing with key issues concerning black lives and ministry. What had begun as meetings for black students only had to be expanded to accommodate the interests of majority students who would not be denied. Something was clearly afoot during those days, and by the time Skinner began his speech the place was buzzing with anticipation. The evening speech was electric. Most of us had not been impacted by a single sermon such as he delivered in all our lives. When he closed, the place erupted with a standing ovation of enormous power. Something had happened. As Skinner himself proclaimed in conclusion, "The Liberator has come!"

David Howard was the heartbeat of InterVarsity missions. He was a missionary himself and had served fifteen years in Colombia. For five decades he would coordinate the Urbana conferences.

We had met before, but our meeting after Urbana '70 was different. We were on the same plane. I enjoyed his company and learned a good deal about the work of the Spirit in South America listening to him. But then we got to talking about Urbana and what had happened there, and I realized that he harbored a deep-seated concern. He was still fearful that the issue of justice threatened the ministry of foreign missions as it had been championed and practiced through IV since the mid-forties. It would have been one thing if black students had responded to Tom's sermon with wild enthusiasm, but when the majority of students there who were white had responded with unprecedented support—well, that was something else. He didn't spell it out as clearly as this, but it was there. He needed some sort of assurance that black Christians were not going to hijack missions. I tried to offer that.

If Skinner's sermon at Urbana proved to be a problem with some of the leadership at InterVarsity, it also served to call Tom Skinner Associates to rethink its theology. Skinner's sermon at Urbana seemed to require of the organization that we rethink our theological stance. If liberation was a key motif in Scripture, and certainly in the minds and actions of many in the civil rights movement, where was it to be found in our work? Was conversion to Christ the same as liberation? And was conversion to Christ intended to move one from self-centeredness to a more social expression of the changed life?

The team met in our Brooklyn office for a team meeting and there decided that the time had come for us to unpack the New Testament emphasis upon the kingdom of God. We were being criticized for becoming too "radical" as defined by what was happening in movements within the larger society; we decided to take the term and baptize it in New Testament holy water. We would become radicals indeed only as defined by Christ's teaching about his kingdom. This would not please our supporters from the Plymouth Brethren tradition, whose theology required an emphasis on the church, not the kingdom; neither would it please, as it turned out, a large segment of the evangelical community. It would certainly not have pleased the lady from Newark.

18

Sleeping Through a Revolution

One of the challenges associated with my work with Skinner Associates was the time spent away from home. This had always been problematic, since it was one thing to be single as an evangelist and another thing to be married with children. Hazel understood my obligations associated with our ministries here and there and our team meetings at the office in Brooklyn. She was more understanding than Skinner was. He seemed not to understand why I would head for the airport as soon as the last item was dealt with at the meeting. I could get a late afternoon or early evening flight out of LaGuardia and be home the same night. He wanted me to stay over for the evening and head out the next morning.

I never understood his thinking. After all, he was married at the time and had two lovely daughters. He lived nearby as a crow would fly, just around the corner from the office, and I assumed that he would be anxious to get home after a busy week. But then we were to learn that things were not going well with his marriage, and it gradually was terminated in divorce. Perhaps what he wanted from me was companionship for the evening. I may have been insensitive to his needs, but I was homesick, and emotionally drained. It was time to go home, and I was anxious to get going.

I had been busy in ministries since our marriage. More than I realized. This was due in part to the fact that we needed the money. The remuneration from this sort of work was usually in the form of what was called a "love offering," or a free will offering, and it could vary from church to church. Sometimes it could be substantial, and the elders of the church would hold back part of it, without telling me, of course. But we needed the money even though Hazel was working. Then the children came along. It wasn't until I agreed to work with Skinner that I received a salary. It was a relief, but it also felt a bit strange, like a betrayal of faith. The feeling went away fairly soon.

I recall backing out of our driveway on the way to an assignment among some churches in Michigan. Paul from Cedine Bible Camp had suffered a mild collapse as we sat together with the Nottages. He had come to the state to raise money for the ministry. I had volunteered to finish his itinerary. But leaving the family that evening proved to be too much. Philip was beginning to drive, and he and Peter were working through the trauma of a school system struggling to right itself after one of the city's worst riots. I wondered who would take care of the boys if I was gone so much. I was upset and thought that I should have stayed home. I wept softly as I drove up the street. It was then that I heard the Spirit say to me, "I took care of you, didn't I?" Indeed, he had, and by the time I reached the freeway I had been bathed in his peace. Every preacher I had met had the same story, and not all of their marriages survived their frequent absences. Marriages faltered, children became alienated, some from the faith as well as from the family.

One night during my time with Skinner Associates, the phone rang. I reached across the table in the kitchen nook, took the phone in hand, and heard Kenneth Kantzer's voice. I knew who he was and that his work at Wheaton and *Christianity Today* magazine was stellar. He was calling from his office at Trinity Evangelical Divinity School to ask if I would consider joining the faculty there. Ours was a very warm chat, and I told him that I didn't think I could leave Skinner Associates at the time. We had work laid out ahead of us that had to be finished. Then he asked if I would consider teaching a course or two. I could commute from Detroit. I agreed to consider that, and we began to shape courses that would expose Trinity students to the black experience. Broadly stated, they would be courses about the black church in an urban world.

The series at Trinity went well, and the students were ready to listen to my focus. Several of the white students were more interested than others.

One was a young red-haired man with a full beard, who held out his hand and introduced himself as Jim Wallis. I had met Jim when he was a teenager. He belonged to the Brethren Assemblies in suburban Detroit. He had been upset by the distance between black and white believers in that movement and had sought me out to vent his concerns. He then disappeared from my sight and buried himself in the student movement against the war in Vietnam. When that movement came apart, he was thrust back to the Scriptures. With a new lens honed from his peace movement activities, he saw a different Jesus. He and his associates would drive me to O'Hare after class during my time at Trinity, and we'd laugh and talk. It was the only time in all my travels that I was content when a flight was delayed. They told me that they had decided to move their operations from nearby Wheaton to Washington. I thought that that was interesting since *Christianity Today*, the journalistic mouthpiece for the evangelical movement, had decided to move from Washington to Wheaton.

The other phone call of significance came from Chicago. The voice on the other end was an acquaintance from my days in Youth for Christ. Russ Reid had been a pioneer in advertising for Christian ministries. While many of us thought him to be out to lunch in the beginning, he had proven us wrong. I was surprised to hear his voice, since we had not been close. After the usual pleasantries he said, "Bill, I have been watching the funeral of Dr. King, and I realize that I have slept through a revolution. I have no idea of this man's significance." I was taken aback by his admission, and then he said, "Would you be willing to come over here and spend a day telling us what we slept through? I'll fly you over, of course."

Hazel reluctantly agreed that this would be an important meeting. Russ picked me up in his British-green Chrysler sedan, and I spent the day with him and his team. It went well, and Russ and I became longtime friends.

What my friend and evangelical brother did not know was that the entire evangelical movement had slept through a revolution. This was due partly to the civil rights movement being based in the South. Evangelicalism was anchored in the North and Northeast, and in the West at Fuller Seminary in Pasadena. It was white and rooted in the history of fundamentalism and revivalism. That accounted for some of the deafness of evangelical leaders when it came to the preaching of Dr. King. They did not hear the clear-cut soundings of the gospel calling people to repent and be saved. There was no sawdust trail in King's ministry, no revivalism. Then too, the Southern Christian Leadership Conference was black. Strike two. There was the question of whether Rev. King was really preaching the gospel. He seemed to be talking about Jesus, but this was surely not the Jesus of Moody, nor of Sankey, Sunday, or Graham. It was one thing to rejoice in the musical ministry of the Fisk Jubilee Singers; it was another thing for white evangelicals to hear the good news of a gospel that called America to repent of the sins of discrimination and racism. Before the advent of so-called civil rights, there was the challenge to segregated schools in *Brown v. Board of Education of Topeka*. But that too was southern in origin and in application. Only later did it rear its ugly head in the North.

Chicago had become a key city for any movement concerned with reaching the rest of the country. It was a key location for Martin King's attack on racism and segregation in the North. It was also a key city for the growing ministry of Billy Graham. And it was certainly the centerpiece of the display of power politics that modeled the clash between power and powerlessness in America's urban centers. The voice and face of that clash was Mayor Richard J. Daley. America had become an urban country, and white America was having a difficult time adjusting. The difficulty took many forms, but the major adjustment was their abandonment of the core of these great cities. Years later, as the impact of Billy Graham's revivalism had lost much of its energy, his meetings were held in suburban centers as white Christians were wary of venturing downtown for meetings. Why risk being mobbed in downtown Detroit when you can worship comfortably in a cozy setting in Pontiac? Even the Detroit Pistons had abandoned downtown Detroit. They played their games in the safe confines of suburban Auburn Hills. So also, the Lions in football. Only the baseball team stayed downtown. Hooray for the Tigers! I was connected with the Detroit chapter of evangelicals and once served as the treasurer. On one occasion I inquired about a scheduled meeting and learned that it had been moved. It was no longer in the city, but farther out, near a suburban community. That's when I learned that key congregations had moved almost overnight to such locations. They simply vanished from view. The evangelical movement in the city was now in the hands of non-white believers, and these urbanites knew, beyond knowing, that the cultural significance of urban America was power.

Among all the key urban centers in America, no city, outside New York perhaps, could match Chicago as a place defined by raw power. Ralph Abernathy, in his deeply personal account of his partnership with Dr. King, admitted that their preparation for entry into Chicago was woefully inadequate. "We entered a different world when we came to this northern city in 1966, a world we didn't fully understand." What they didn't understand was that Chicago was "the Birmingham of the North," and before the smoke had cleared on their efforts, it was painfully clear that the Southern Christian Leadership Conference should have stayed in the South. Abernathy confessed that the battering the team had suffered in Chicago was so thorough that, in his opinion, his friend Martin never recovered from it.

Chicago had become important to King before his attempt to take it on in 1966. It was here that he met the noted Jewish scholar and theologian Abraham Heschel. They had been delegates at the National Conference on Religion and Race in 1963. It was here that these two giants of culture, prophecy, and ecumenicity forged a relationship that set the tone of religious leadership for years to come. It would take evangelicals several years to stage a similar gathering, a minor blip on the ecumenical landscape. The conference came to be known as the Thanksgiving Workshop on Evangelicals and Social Concern.

The invitation to consider an evangelistic crusade in Chicago came from a black businessman. We had completed meetings in Patterson, New Jersey, and in Copiague, Long Island, following the series in Newark. We were encouraged by the receptions we were receiving from various churches and evangelical leaders to consider coming to their cities. But momentum can be a dangerous thing, especially if one's organization or ministry is in the growing stages. Had we been more aware of this, we might not have been so prepared to consider the overture we received from Chicago. Mr. Hayes, the businessman who had invited us, was connected with key pastors in the black communities of South Chicago and selected Dr. Wilbur Daniel to head up the event. Daniel was the pastor of Antioch Baptist Church, one of the South Side's larger and more influential congregations. I represented the team initially. A committee had been selected, an all-male gathering of businessmen and pastors.

Skinner had hired Richard Parker as our frontman to organize the crusades. Richard was a person gifted at working with people. Skinner found him in a holiness church in Philadelphia and the backroom of a local pharmacy. Tom had prepared Richard for his work, and Chicago was his first assignment. I had not met him before. Skinner had assured him that I had completed the preliminary work in preparation for the series. Nothing could have been further from the truth. I not only had not done this work, but I really had no idea how it should be done. I had been in and out of Chicago for many years. We had relatives there, and my father lived in Morgan Park. All I knew about that great city was that I knew very little about it. In fact, we were naive in the extreme. We should have known better than to attempt such a series. We were understaffed, underfunded, and largely ignorant of the dynamics of Chicago's South Side. We did not know who the real players among the pastors were. Many people, black and white, thought of us as black versions of Billy Graham. Others came to think of us as evangelical versions of Operation Breadbasket, Jesse Jackson's attempt to bring healing to the area on Saturday mornings.

Richard arrived in Chicago on a cold day in January 1970. He did not know that Chicago weather, fresh off the icy shore of Lake Michigan, was quite different from the winter weather in Philadelphia. He was to stay at the Center for Continuing Education, but his first decision was to buy a pair or two of long underwear. What followed was to be the ongoing experience of his fledgling career. In conversation with me and others on the committee, he learned that very little had been done to organize the crusade. Skinner was misinformed, and I was waiting for our bright, new employee to get us going. We had secured the Coliseum for two weeks beginning in April. It seated six thousand people. Fools rush in. After we got Richard settled in the Center for Continuing Education building, it was time to talk about our progress in organizing the crusade. He was startled, upset, and confused when I recited my experience in the city and my relations with the committee. He told me that Skinner had told him that we were all but set to begin the series, and I was confused since Tom and I had not had that conversation. Richard was stunned and realized that he had to begin preparations from scratch by getting his bearings among churches and small groups of interested organizations in the city. Skinner and I busied ourselves in speaking engagements among churches and colleges. We were pleased to accept an overture from the Graham people to consider assistance from them. The dinner was very nice; the soup, gazpacho, was delicious. Graham's representative engaged us in the usual evangelistic palaver with which we were familiar but then proceeded to suggest that what we were attempting was probably beyond our capacity to attain.

He was right when viewed from the perspective of the Graham organization and experience. They were connected in ways we had not imagined. But were we also an irritant, however minor? Was our presence a potential obstacle to their plans for the city? We assured our host that we were grateful for his counsel but that we were prepared to move ahead with our plans for the South Side. We knew that we could not possibly present an impediment to any plans our colleagues were planning. Was this another incident intended to remind us that there were people who wanted us to succeed, but not too well?

The Coliseum was nearly full each night of our series. It was an intramural event, a series that was black and South Side from the beginning, just as we had planned it.

Leona Bunch with Bill and his sister Beverly (date unknown)

Young Bill riding on a pony, (toy) guns blazing (summer of 1935)

Bill with his mother, Olive, and three of his siblings (May 30, 1936)

Bill with his sister Beverly and Aunt Edna (his mother's sister) during a trip to Chicago that was Beverly's first time meeting their father (date unknown)

Bill (date unknown)

Bill (date unknown)

B. M. Nottage, with Bill, relaxing on a Michigan beach (date unknown)

Bill and Hazel on their wedding day (October 15, 1955)

Hazel on their wedding day (October 15, 1955)

Bill with Philip (approx. 1959)

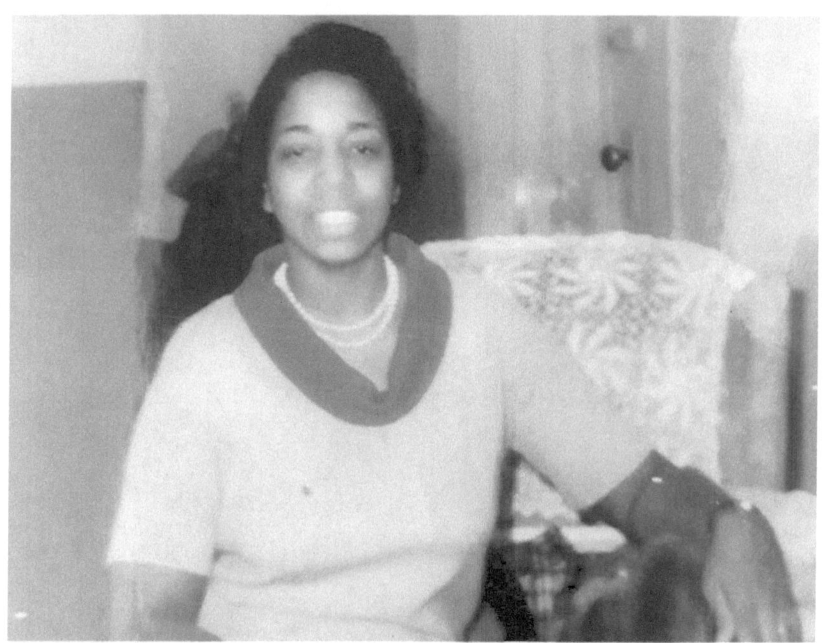

Hazel (approx. 1968)

Bill (date unknown)

Bill and Hazel on her ninety-fifth birthday (February 14, 2019)

PART 3

Fuller Theological Seminary: 1974–2014

19

A Life-Changing Invitation

IN THE SUMMER OF 1971, an invitation came that was to change both the vocation and location of my evangelistic ministry. David Hubbard, the president of Fuller Theological Seminary in Pasadena, California, invited me to meet him in the American Airlines Admirals Club at the Detroit International Airport.

I had met Dr. Hubbard in Berlin in 1966 on a bus transporting us from the World Congress on Evangelism to our hotel. I had just finished a conversation with Oral Roberts, who had invited me to an upcoming pastor's conference at Oral Roberts University and assured me that I would be welcome. Blessed assurance.

When I heard my name mentioned, I turned, shook Dr. Hubbard's extended hand, and felt the warmth of his smile. "Hi," he said. "I'm David Hubbard from Fuller Seminary in Pasadena." (I was to learn later from his secretary, Inez Smith, that Dr. Hubbard did not respond well if one were to refer to him as Dave.) Ours was scarcely a conversation, more like a brief exchange of pleasantries.

The next time I heard that voice was at the Admirals Club in Detroit. It was the same warm sound I had heard in Berlin, and the same firm handshake. Our eyes met and I knew it was going to be all right, whatever the occasion.

To my surprise, President Hubbard invited me to join the board of trustees of Fuller Seminary. I did not know it at the time, but Dr. Hubbard became well known for his leadership in building board memberships. His conversation with me had to do with making sure the seminary moved beyond being a lily-white institution. "We have come to believe that we cannot represent the kingdom with integrity if we remain a monocultural institution."

I was impressed. I had had conversations with evangelical executives over the years, from colleges to mission executives, but this was the first executive who pitched my services in a theological context.

Recovering from his invitation, I thought it necessary to confess that I had no money to bring to such a post. He was quick to assure me that he knew that. He then assured me that he thought I possessed other gifts that the school needed.

When we parted company that day, I knew I had been directed westward. However, I wasn't certain about Hazel's response to my report about that meeting. She seemed pleased, and since it didn't entail a move, it was all right that I accept the invitation to join the board.

The board met in the stately rooms at the Huntington Hotel in Pasadena (now the Langham Huntington). It was a landmark edifice with large rooms, lavishly decorated. A far, far cry from Holiday Inns with which I was familiar. But what made these meetings memorable was an invitation from Max De Pree to be his roommate.

De Pree was an American businessman who assumed the leadership of the Herman Miller office furniture company in the early 1960s. He was credited with turning a small family-owned business into what was at the time the second largest furniture maker in the world. His book *Leadership Is an Art* (1987) focused on the need for covenantal relationships within organizations, where all voices are heard, and people are bound to one another and enabled to meet corporate needs through meeting the needs of one another.

De Pree sensed that I was lost among the members, and probably in over my head. He was right. I didn't realize it at the time, but I was to learn from Max just how foundational a board was to an institution. Indeed, if you show me your board, I'll show you your institution.

I was also to learn from Max how gifted board leadership, married to warm spiritual integrity, could cement a lifelong friendship. Max introduced me to his wife, Esther, and together they invited Hazel and the boys to share their home on weekends. With their daughter, we enjoyed touch football in their yard, along with all the goodies that went with their hospitality.

We would remain tight friends long after we both retired from the seminary. Both of us grew up in Michigan. There were times when I thought he and I were probably the only Democrats in that part of western Michigan.

President Hubbard and De Pree shaped Fuller's board. Together they held conferences on the craft of board building. Hubbard provided the theology necessary for board shaping; Max provided the broad experience necessary to ensure that board members and faculty worked in harmony. The two men were fast and deep friends.

I had the good sense to keep my comments at the initial board meetings to a bare minimum, but I knew that what I was learning in Pasadena I could bring with me back to our work at Tom Skinner Associates.

My final series with the Skinner team was in Florida in 1973. Rich Parker had done his usual fine work in setting up the series, and we arrived in the city quite ready to proceed. An evening social was planned, to which the team and local participants from the city were invited. It would be followed by the kick-off session with Tom preaching.

The only problem with the arrangement was Tom's absence. He was not present in the afternoon, nor at the evening social. I tried to locate him, beginning in the morning, but received no replies to my calls. I decided to try one more time, and this time he replied to my phone call.

I went to his room, and we had what would prove to be our last conversation about the organization and our place in it. I had thought for some time that Tom had all but departed the team months before. He was our absent colleague. We were more likely to see him on the sidelines of a Redskins football game than at team meetings that would chart our future. Tom was gifted and effective in his ministry with professional athletes.

I knew after the Florida series that, for me at least, there would be no future in the organization. The series in St. Petersburg went well. As usual, Tom's preaching was well received. The efforts by other members of the team and by local leaders proved fruitful. The auditorium was filled nightly, and there was the usual encouraging response to the gospel message. Richard was especially pleased to see all the hard work he had done result in such fruitfulness.

I returned home the morning following the last night of the meetings. After the usual warm greetings with the kids and Hazel, I began to share with her how the event went and my experience with Tom. I told her that it would be my final meeting with the association.

She was not surprised. She had known for some months that I was not happy with my work there. If I was unhappy, she was unhappy.

The next question had to do with our future. I knew I could stay in Detroit and work with the congregations that made up our "Brethren network." I could have become a younger version of Mr. Nottage since I had somehow become his anointed son.

This did not suit Hazel. She did not see me in that role. Besides, she doubted that I would be good at conflict management. I had learned early in our marriage that Hazel often knew better than me what might be good for the chapters in my ministry.

In this case, she had been part of the congregation's life longer than I, and she could put faces on those conflicts. Nottage and I had spoken of these challenges, but then I was still living out of a suitcase.

After some period at home, I thought it was time, and perhaps safe, to remind Hazel of the invitation I had received from the leadership at Fuller Seminary. On a couple of occasions, the seminary had let me know that if I was ever to lean into the possibility of faculty or academic work, they would be pleased if I gave them a chance to speak with me before I went someplace else.

Hazel knew about this but was not prepared to think that I would really consider moving to Pasadena. Being a member of the board there for some years was one thing, but moving there, living out there, leaving Detroit, well, that was something else.

There was considerable unrest in Detroit. The riots of 1967 had torn the city apart; this upheaval seemed to be far worse than previous disturbances. We had become accustomed to disturbances in the city, almost all of them clashes between white cops from Hamtramck, who were poorly trained, and black men within the city. This one was deeper and more widespread. This one would result in the final departure of whites and Jews from the city. This one would eventually redefine Detroit as America's leading black city.

The unrest was particularly hard on young people, and we had two of them in our house. We wondered about their future as they faced high school, and we stewed over where we should send them as they finished junior high and high school respectively. Maybe religious schools, Catholic or Lutheran. In one way, a move to California seemed to be an attractive one.

But there were all our friends, the young people from the churches, the guys who ended up at our house to shoot hoops in the backyard. Then there were the ladies of the fellowship with whom Hazel had established warm relations over the years, and teachers from Sunday school and youth groups—too much to walk away from.

We decided to send a letter to Provost Glenn Barker agreeing to speak with the Fuller people at the next board meeting. I told them that I was leaning toward some sort of academic life and that I wanted to study. I also wanted to spend more time with the boys. They listened, of course, and then assured me that they would be in touch.

Their response was immediate. They offered me a faculty position teaching evangelism and said they would fly Hazel and me to Pasadena to look for housing. The ball was in our court.

I had one more evangelistic meeting to attend. I was to share the platform at the final conference of the season at Maranatha Bible Conference near Muskegon, Michigan.

I would share the platform with Richard Halverson, pastor of the Fourth Presbyterian Church in Washington, DC. Dr. Halverson was part of the celebrated group of Presbyterian men who had been tutored by the legendary Henrietta Mears of the Hollywood Presbyterian Church in Southern California. They had become well known, especially among the more conservative Presbyterian churches across the land. I had worked with some of them when we met under the auspices of Faith at Work. I had preached in Bethlehem, Pennsylvania, for Lloyd Ogilvie the weekend he was in Los Angeles meeting with the elders of Hollywood Presbyterian about becoming their pastor. These connections would lead both men further into Republican politics as both, in their turn, were selected to become chaplains of the United States Senate.

Halverson and I had been in a conversation for the greater part of a year prior to the Maranatha event. He was the author of a very nice devotional in which he wrote about current affairs from biblical perspectives.

When he began a short series suggesting that the apostle Paul spent no time in his career urging the churches to demonstrate against the injustices of their time, I wrote to suggest otherwise. The times had changed since the apostle's letters, I reasoned, and the call to demonstrate in the service of justice during a time when there was a church on every corner was well within the parameters of good discipleship.

We disagreed. He was most pleasant in our paper exchanges, as he was on the day we shared the pulpit. He could afford to be. We parted the day in good spirits, but I never saw him again.

20

A New Kind of Evangelical Seminary

While I was preaching in Muskegon, Hazel was busy putting the final touches on the business negotiations that would free us to move to California. We were not too happy with the price we received for the house. We were even more unhappy about the amount we were to pay for our new dwelling in Altadena.

Our realtor was very helpful. He showed us houses all over the east side of Altadena, suggesting that it would be wise to choose a place with either a pool or air conditioning. Both options were strange to us, since we had neither in our homes in Detroit. We chose air conditioning. We opted to buy on the east side of Altadena even though it meant we would be the only black family in the area.

The possibility of black people buying on the east side was a recent one, due to the passage of a law that prevented banks and realtors from refusing to sell to black people east of Lake Avenue, the street that separated the city east and west.

I thought it would be a good idea to buy where we did in case the job at the seminary didn't work past the initial three years. It would be easier for us to sell the place from the east side than from the west, even though people of color lived on the west side.

But why Fuller? Fuller Theological Seminary was not the only evangelical seminary in the country. It wasn't the only seminary I had visited as a guest speaker. All these schools related to their Christian college counterparts and shared an interlocking network of board members. I had become familiar with this network, and in a sense was part of it. I knew that there were certain colleges and seminaries where I was not welcome. Those doors were not slammed shut, just closed with a gentle click.

This had become especially evident as a result of the release of my book *My Friend, the Enemy*, in 1968. I was aware that these schools were looking for their kind of "negro," one they could live with, someone with impeccable theological credentials who would not make waves contrary to the school's theological or cultural traditions.

When word got around that I had become a member of Fuller's faculty, members of other evangelical schools would not have been surprised. It figured. Well, yes, it was their attitude toward Fuller that drew me to the place.

When a member of the faculty of Gordon-Conwell Theological Seminary, located in Hamilton, Massachusetts, a suburb of Boston, asked me why I had gone to Fuller, I replied, "They asked me."

He wasn't pleased with my answer, not that Gordon was prepared to ask if I was available. But then there were flirtations all over the place in those days. Most evangelical schools were flirting with hiring a black faculty member. One.

By the time Fuller invited me to join the faculty, I had visited a number of evangelical schools. I had served on boards here and there among evangelical ministries. I had been involved in discussions with mission executives about their policies and practices that might or might not account for the absence of black members in those ministries. The same could be said about all the other black evangelicals of this generation. We knew each other, and when we got together, we would swap stories about the games that were being played, who played them, and what the future might be if we went here, there, or nowhere among these groups. Most of us decided that we would choose to be among those white evangelicals who would not expect us to be invisible.

I was impressed with the location of the seminary. When founder Charles Fuller had selected a location for the new school, he seemed to have decided to line it up with the city's political offices. It would be safe from any future encroachment of traffic lanes. It would be located near the heart of the city. Los Angeles was only ten miles away. The seminary would be an urban school, even though such a category was probably not in use at the time.

Places such as Trinity Evangelical Divinity School seemed far removed from the future of American cities. Its constituencies had already begun to abandon the cities, especially Chicago, and the school would scarcely be a model of urban involvement to students. I didn't intend to be stuck in the suburbs, a black family with two kids in high school living in a suburb where we would be one of the few blacks living there.

Fuller's faculty was a major attraction. As a young preacher, I had read Everett Harrison's essays in *Christianity Today*. There was a fine spirit in his writing, a warmth that seemed to embrace his understanding of the Bible as the word of God, unlike the usual scholarly exposition of its defense. When I met him, I discovered the same spirit in the man: gentle, warm, and deeply devotional. Students would take his classes just to hear his devotional prayers that launched each class.

I knew of George Eldon Ladd's pathbreaking book *The Gospel of the Kingdom* (1959). I had learned about early pioneers whose agitation had provoked the beginnings of the school. If I had become a fundamentalist under the influence of early revivalists and the holiness movement, I later became an evangelical under the long-range influence of Carl F. H. Henry, Harold John Ockenga, and the radio preaching of Charles E. Fuller.

As an evangelical seminary in contrast to a fundamentalist seminary, Fuller had sounded a different note, the possibility of a seminary that throbbed with a more contemporary relevance.

To join the Fuller faculty, I had to take the seminary's theology exam. This was a requisite procedure, and my examiners were distinguished members of the theology faculty.

I had met Paul Jewett many years before at a black evangelical gathering in Cleveland. I knew Geoffrey Bromiley only by his reputation as a premier historian of the Christian tradition. I knew Glenn Barker from our budding friendship when I was a guest at Gordon-Conwell, where he had been dean before coming to Fuller. Barker, as dean of Fuller's school of theology, served as the host of the theology exam.

Somewhere in that discussion, the issue of the inerrancy of the Bible surfaced. Inerrancy was to become the heart of the so-called battle for the Bible some years later. I gave a response that seemed to bounce off the minds of Bromiley and Jewett. They clearly were not in sync with my answer, and it was easy for me to listen to these two scholars discuss my reply. They forgot me for a few minutes, and I was pleased. Later Dr. Barker remarked that I knew more theology than other evangelists he knew. I passed the exam and was officially on my way.

The issue of my understanding of Scripture surfaced again during a faculty meeting. It may have been triggered by a faculty member's awareness that I was coming to Fuller as an evangelist. I had noted that one of my early champions of Pauline teaching was the Scottish preacher James Stewart, through his book on a Pauline understanding of the believer's life, *A Man in Christ*. Dr. Ralph Martin, from England, seemed pleased with my answer, not because he agreed with it, but because it reflected study on the issue. The faculty would not mistake me for a scholar, but at least I made it less easy for them to dismiss me as a somewhat lightweight evangelist. And a Yankee to boot.

But the faculty was not a place in which to get warm. I did not sense that the key players, the veterans, had time to be friendly, or in academic terms, collegial. I did not doubt their spirituality. All of them were members of local congregations. What seemed to be missing was any serious attempt to be friendly, warm, and, I dare say, loving. This was a very busy group, and the doors of their offices were not usually open for friendly chats. Maybe they had decided to leave all that warm-fuzzy stuff to their wives.

Years before Hazel and I arrived in Pasadena, they had formed a fellowship group of faculty wives, even giving it a name and electing officers. Eventually, Hazel became a partner of this fellowship.

But she never felt at home when the faculty and wives got together. She never felt that the wives group as a whole got to the level of real life in the meetings. Hazel was really about her family, her husband, and the children. Whatever else faculty types did, whatever achievements they represented, that was fine with her. But too often those were the topics in meetings, and she preferred to stay home. "When do these people get real?" was her continuing question.

But I did come to know something of the warm and friendly side of these men. I recall discussing Stanford University football with Geoffrey Bromiley. Later I told him about an invitation to accept an honorary doctorate degree from a Christian university. I knew the difference between an earned doctorate and an honorary degree. I knew that honorary degrees did not carry the same weight as earned degrees. I might have been comfortable in my experience as an evangelist, but I knew of no school where one could earn a doctorate in evangelism. I was intimidated.

Bromiley listened carefully and then told me that all things being equal, anybody could earn a doctorate. But to receive an honorary degree was something different and special. It had to do with recognition and merit in one's field and in service to the Christian enterprise. His counsel gave me fresh insight and made a great difference in my acceptance of the degree some months later.

Bromiley was a pacifist and a teetotaler. He was also a hiker, and the local mountain trails were an important part of his habitat. I came to regard him as a godly man, but as one who grew up and was educated in England, his display of his faith was largely a private matter.

The faculty was productive. They did research and wrote books. They authored articles in respected journals. This was a theological faculty. I was not surprised. After all, it was a theological seminary. Furthermore, it was a faculty that thoroughly understood and bought into the school's reason to be. They weren't playing games about why the school existed, what was at stake in the future of the evangelical movement. Fundamentalism may have needed to be reformed, but if that was to be accomplished, it needed a new and more sophisticated theological foundation. This was a theological faculty. They happily left the work of evangelism and Christian education to others. I felt this commitment; this was where I wanted to be, and I knew that somewhere down the line I would go back to school.

In an interview with a campus magazine, Dr. Hubbard candidly discussed his attraction to the seminary as he considered becoming its third president. His reasons were vintage Hubbard, but I was especially attracted to his inner sense that Fuller was "a school the Lord had chosen to be influential."

This would sum up my own attraction to the place. I knew that my departure from the churches in Detroit was not well received by some of the leaders among the black Brethren church network. After all, Bethany was the mother congregation, and Nottage was gone. It was the key pulpit within the network. As one leader put it when he heard I was leaving, "There are all sorts of other people who can do evangelism at Fuller."

He was right if doing evangelism was all I had in mind. But what I had in mind was influence, making it possible for Fuller to become the most influential center for anyone interested in impacting the future of the black church in America.

21

What Would Be My Place at Fuller?

PROVOST BARKER DIDN'T QUITE know what to do with me. I was the first individual Fuller hired to teach evangelism and the first African American member of the faculty.

Barker was something of a hustler. He was warm and friendly, and we became friends. He was a fine scholar and Bible teacher. He was a family man with three children, two girls and a boy. His wife, Margaret, was a splendid complement. She laughed easily. She and Hazel would become good friends.

Glenn was a competitor, whether on campus, or playing touch football, or swinging a golf club. So when he approached me about working with Dr. Robert Munger, I wasn't certain what he had in mind. He told me that Munger was probably the most important connection he had with students.

Munger was a Presbyterian who had served as pastor of two large, influential Presbyterian congregations in Berkeley, California, and Seattle, Washington. At that time, most of our students were from the evangelical wing of the Presbyterian denomination.

I had "met" Robert Boyd Munger while driving across the southern tip of Chicago. His voice on Moody Radio and his sermon "My Heart—Christ's Home" celebrated the mystical union of Christ and the believer, but in a way that was somehow less complicated. The sermon became a classic. At Fuller, I would have the pleasure of working together with him to assist students in practicing a winsome evangelism.

Munger's passion wasn't evangelism, although he was committed to its practice. Sort of. His real passion was the renewal of the local congregation. He knew that most Presbyterian congregations would never embrace evangelism unless they experienced some form of spiritual renewal.

Munger's method was to develop teams of students and send them out to work with congregations, exposing them to his understanding of the necessity and practice of renewal. He developed exercises to assist small groups, and he trained students in these tactics. Munger was a hot item on campus. But he was also in great demand among churches on weekends, and he would not consent to preach unless he could bring a team of students with him.

I was a newcomer. I had a reputation as an evangelist. Barker knew I could teach, but the hot button on campus was not a class in evangelism; it was Munger's teaching about small groups in which personal sharing of Christian experience and prayer would be prominent. Provost Barker asked if I could work with Munger. "Can you do what Munger is doing?" I told him I could. I had done much of the same work with Faith at Work for some years prior to coming to Fuller. Those meetings were largely Presbyterian and Episcopalian in makeup.

Small groups as a strategy to engage believers in discipleship was becoming more popular in ministries across the land in the 1970s. But the practice could be traced back to the Wesleyan movement in England, and to similar revival movements in America.

The Methodists called them "class meetings," and they were the core settings for everything from Bible study to church discipline. Munger did not go this far in his work, and it was probably a good thing. There was a considerable distance between what Methodists practiced and what Presbyterians could handle. In all fairness, much of contemporary Methodism wasn't working all that well within their own traditions.

I enjoyed my work with Munger, but I grew weary of the games we were playing in our attempts to get congregants to loosen up and enjoy life in the Spirit. I think I was too Wesleyan. I thought that I knew what revival looked like and sounded like. My early experiences in revival meetings were of the summer camp meeting genre, almost all within the holiness or Methodist traditions. I had read some of the nineteenth-century evangelist Charles W. Finney's classic lectures on revival, and even sought to practice some of his insights in my preaching. It was this combination of revival and reform that had given birth to the college at Oberlin, Ohio, of which Finney became president.

But it was a Mennonite pastor who introduced me to another movement, this one from England, that had a different attraction for me. I was preaching in a Mennonite church in Ohio, and its pastor, Gerald C. Studer, asked me if I had ever heard of the Oxford Group movement. I remarked that I had not, and he proceeded to give me a book that chronicled this remarkable outworking of the Spirit at this citadel of academic sophistication and upper crust culture.

Later, as I began to work with my friend Gene Herr, a visionary leader in the Mennonite Church, I learned that he also had heard of this history and of the impact it had on Sam Shoemaker, a well-known minister of Calvary Episcopal Church in Pittsburgh. Shoemaker had worked with Frank Buchman, the early leader of the Oxford Group. He had met Buchman in China and became a leader of the movement while a pastor of Calvary Episcopal Church in New York City. Gene had been influenced by Shoemaker's ministry.

The final connection with the movement came when Gene became acquainted with one of the last members of the group, Sherwood Day, or "Sherry," as he was affectionately called in the movement. I met Sherry and enjoyed his easy laughter and godly spirit. He even shared with us his embarrassment at having fallen in love, a surprise for a man of his advanced age. He married a younger woman, as we all hoped he would. Gene and I began to work with some of the ideas of the group and were fascinated by the stories the elderly man recited.

The key to the movement was the willingness of the group to test everything by four absolutes: absolute love to all, absolute purity, absolute unselfishness, and absolute honesty.

Gene began to organize young people in small groups across the country and to introduce them to these four absolutes. Of course, Mennonite young people were already aware of the centrality of love and matters of honesty and purity. But these values took on a different urgency when made part of small group discipline; they took on a deeper value and challenge when failure was to be admitted and confessed among one's peers.

Mennonite Youth Fellowship took on a different tone under Herr's leadership. Young people, proud of their heritage, were now opting for a deeper and more personal life with the Spirit and one another. It was a beginning, and over the next several years there seemed to be a deeper spiritual core of young people being raised up across the country.

As I moved on to citywide ministries, I forgot about the Oxford Group. Frank Buchman changed its name to Moral Re-Armament in an attempt to widen its appeal to all faiths for a moral and spiritual awakening.

But I was haunted by the dynamism of the Oxford Group during my work with Munger. I became concerned about our inability to lead congregations into intimacy in love and forgiveness, which accounted for my growing lack of enthusiasm. We had small groups, played games, and sang choruses, but we largely failed to experience life together. I had to admit this was hard to do in a weekend.

In 1971, my first year on the board of trustees, President Hubbard appointed a Black Advisory Committee. I was very impressed with this group of pastors from Pasadena and Los Angeles. The committee recommended the launch of two classes for black pastors.

The important one was a writing class.

A year later this committee launched a theological studies program for black clergy. The first class numbered fifteen pastors.

In the fall of 1974, I was appointed as the director of this program. I was not happy. I did not come to Fuller to direct this or any other program. I knew my limitations. I was not a manager and would never have left Detroit to become one.

I had let Barker know of my disappointment. His style was to listen carefully and encouragingly, usually over some ice cream at a nice place around the corner on Colorado Boulevard.

I felt supported in my work in evangelism, but had I been snookered? Here was Barker with his pitch to lead the new program, with Hubbard's support, but their professed encouragement that I join the faculty was as professor of evangelism. I knew that this was a priority with Hubbard. It was part of his unwillingness to head a seminary that was monocultural. I had heard this, and now it was my turn to help promote its happening.

We had scarcely begun the black studies program when I was informed that the school intended to launch a similar program for Hispanic pastors. Nice idea, I thought, if it didn't impede our efforts.

Well, it did. Since the two programs would draw upon the same budgetary stream. We soon learned that the stream was located off campus: The funding for both programs came from the Lilly Foundation in Indianapolis, Indiana.

I had not been at Fuller long before I learned that academics belonged to academies. Each major discipline had its annual gatherings where lectures were held and projects discussed. Old friends clasped hands, hugged each other, and swapped tales associated with their disciplines.

I discovered that professors who taught courses related to evangelism had no such gathering. Seminaries of a more liberal theological bent didn't worry about this lack, for they didn't practice evangelism. Theirs was a commitment to social ethics or matters related to justice issues. A gathering of evangelicals devoted to evangelism seemed to be needed.

This changed in 1973 as several faculty, including the professor of preaching at Princeton Theological Seminary, founded the Academy of Professors of Evangelism (now known as the Academy for Evangelism in Theological Education). As Munger had close connections with Princeton, he was contacted and asked to join. I followed.

22

Finding Our Family Footing in California

In my first years on the faculty at Fuller, I sought to find my identity even as Hazel and our two boys sought to find their identities in a new environment in California, so different than what we had all known in Detroit.

Hazel wanted to find work in a local hospital. She was a professional transcriber and had headed the department at a hospital in Detroit, the first black woman to do so. After we moved to Pasadena, she found a position at a hospital in Los Angeles, but she soon tired of the daily drive. She inquired about a facility in nearby La Cañada, but it didn't seem to be ready for black leadership. Ultimately, she settled in at St. Luke Hospital in Pasadena. It worked well on several levels, not the least being that it was less than a quarter mile from our house.

Our oldest son, Philip, was enrolled at historic John Muir High School on the west side of Pasadena, while Peter attended Elliot Junior High on the north end of the city. They both seemed to make the transitions from Detroit with ease—better than their parents. Once they began to make friends, they never looked back.

My fears that I had done them irreparable damage by moving them across the country for their older years in school seemed not to have been realized. Philip graduated in 1975 and made his way to a local junior college.

About this time, I learned that Whitworth College in Spokane, Washington, was holding a fundraising banquet on Los Angeles's west side. The school had been a favorite of all the Christian schools I had visited, so I arranged to attend the banquet.

At the banquet I learned that the college provided transportation from LA to Spokane to anyone who wanted to check out the school. I had no difficulty in talking Philip into joining the busload of young people from the Southland as they journeyed to Spokane.

The following year witnessed the same event and the same offer of a trip for young people. That year I was the emcee of the banquet. Philip made the bus trip and decided to enroll at Whitworth.

Peter graduated from John Muir in 1980. He became a fine tennis player and with his partner became conference champion in doubles.

In the spring of 1980, I was the speaker at the annual spiritual emphasis week at Point Loma Nazarene College near San Diego. As was my habit, I roamed the campus, taking in the beauty of the place. The campus anchored property that overlooked the Pacific Ocean. As I wandered, I engaged a few students and an occasional faculty member. I liked the place. The organist was a relative of one of my students at Fuller.

The tennis coach confided in me his need for players, and I told him about Peter. He was immediately interested and offered Peter a scholarship.

So, Philip went north to Spokane and Peter went south to San Diego.

One of the unexpected delights in moving to sunny Southern California was the possibility of golf all through the year. The Brookside Golf Course in Pasadena is lovely any time of the year. It was the site of the Los Angeles Open, bringing to the city some of the world's leading professional golfers. For football games, including the Rose Bowl on New Year's Day, it had one of the loveliest parking lots I had ever seen, an eighteen-hole golf course.

I played golf with President Hubbard and Dean Barker. Our talents were nearly identical, none of us likely to break any golfing records. By the early 1980s I had become more than comfortable with these men. We had become friends.

One afternoon at Brookside I was surprised when Hubbard asked about my interest in further education. Both men seemed to share in this inquiry. I confessed that I intended to resume further work. I was pleased to know of their interest, but also a bit unnerved at the forwardness of their inquiry. What were they trying to say? It was enough to mess with a man's golf swing, but was this query tied in any way to my status as a faculty member?

Upon reflection, I realized they weren't attempting anything more than letting me know of their support in the event that I was interested in further study. Hubbard suggested that I consider studying abroad, especially in England. He had studied at St Andrews University in Scotland. He said they were prepared to make it happen.

I was taken aback by their offer and said I would think about it.

But I knew that the prospect of moving to England for studies was not likely. I had had enough of a challenge getting Hazel from Detroit to Pasadena. And now her two kids were in college. Too much.

Hazel confirmed my suspicions, aided, I think, by her perception that I had little interest in moving to England.

Months later I was attracted to a PhD program in social ethics offered at the University of Southern California. USC was just down the freeway in Los Angeles. Neither Hubbard nor Barker ever expressed disappointment with my decision.

My interest in social ethics had begun years earlier when I realized that evangelicals were more comfortable preaching and teaching about personal ethics while the country was being shaken to its foundations by persons and nations caught up in social issues.

There had been the civil rights movement and Vietnam. Even at Fuller there were discussions about the nature of missions and its intersection with theology that fairly dripped with implications for thinking and acting beyond the merely personal.

I knew about Carl Henry's personal ethics and had read his classic book *The Uneasy Conscience of Modern Fundamentalism*. Henry had studied for his doctorate at Boston University. Two years after he began, a young black man entered the school to study Professor Edgar Brightman's theology called "personalism." The student's name was Martin Luther King Jr.

Brightman taught an appreciation of the enduring characteristics and behavior that comprise a person's unique identity in life. Personalism would become a foundation of King's civil rights campaign.

Fuller had been established to break new ground in academic life in order to renew fundamentalism. If successful, it would have a liberating effect on evangelism.

23

Black Theological Studies

WHEN I BECAME THE director of the theological studies program for black pastors, I knew that I needed a more sophisticated understanding of the issues that affected pastoral leadership in the black community. The issues in those communities had everything to do with matters of justice. My challenge was to work on the interface of evangelism and social ethics. Surely justice was more than a mere personal issue. So, in the early eighties I inquired about studying at USC.

As the theological studies program developed, I knew I had to have the black pastors interact with John Perkins, who moved his family to Pasadena in 1982. Born in Mississippi, after leading a movement for voter registration, Perkins was arrested and tortured by white police officers. With his 1976 book *Let Justice Roll Down*, he became one of the leading evangelical voices with an emphasis on racial reconciliation and Christian community development.

In 1982 he established a ministry in northwest Pasadena called Harambee. The word in Swahili means "all pull together."

I had met John in Mendenhall and Jackson, Mississippi, where he established Mendenhall Ministries, before we moved to Fuller. John was becoming something of a legend among white evangelicals because of his achievements in the service of justice and community development in his native state. In the years ahead he would become a safe black man, an alternative who was, for evangelicals, neither a Malcolm X nor a Martin Luther King. King believed strongly in reconciliation, and Jesus was central to his work, a model for his actions. Perkins believed in the same formula, but his understanding of reconciliation didn't drive him to march and demonstrate. For Perkins, Jesus was more than a model. He was a savior, his savior. For Perkins, reconciliation was more than a social issue; it had to do with a new relationship with God. John became a sanctified social worker and an evangelist, a powerful combination in a rather homely black wrapping.

But we didn't belong to the evangelical club. When our friends needed one of us for their major events, we would usually respond. When we gathered among ourselves, we would often laugh at how we were treated, as we seemed to know more about how the game was played than our brothers thought.

John seemed to be less bothered by evangelical behavior than some of us. As the years wore on, he was more in demand, for one thing. John launched his own enterprise, the Christian Community Development Association. He was becoming the face and voice of a new movement that would grow to become the leading Christian development movement in the country.

I was attracted to Perkins's ministry in Pasadena through our friendship. I spoke at some of their events as they developed children's ministries and community outreach. I was especially attracted to the evening gatherings for the neighbors. People from the neighborhood gathered for food and drinks and to discuss the challenges that faced them as a community. The discussions were honest and earnest, and as they grew in number, eventually drew the attention of a local councilman. And that was how they finally got the gang presence across the street cleaned up.

Several years later I thought of that model when reading Robert Wuthnow's *Communities of Discourse: Ideology and Social Structure in the Reformation, the Enlightenment, and European Socialism*, an account of the great movements in Europe that changed the face of that continent politically, economically, and religiously. According to Wuthnow, the changes that effectively saved Europe from social destruction were the gatherings of people who found each other. Not politicians who offered solutions from the top down. A prime example was the Reformation that spawned Protestantism. It emerged from people, ordinary people, not politicians, people who found each other and began to talk, to debate their visions for a new society. Wuthnow called them communities of discourse.

Perkins's program featured three "laws": relocation, reconciliation, and redistribution. His was a strategy that white Christians loved because it seemed to promise a cure for black laziness, or lack of creative enterprise. It was clearly a program that white evangelicals could get behind since it didn't require any marches or demonstrations, and it certainly didn't require that black people move into neighborhoods already occupied by whites.

But it was more than an attempt to please white evangelicals. Relocation, for instance, was a costly option for believers. It was modeled after Jesus himself. Christians called it an incarnation, the Word becoming flesh and dwelling among humans, the Son of God becoming a merciful neighbor. These three practices would become the cornerstones of the development strategy. Under John's leadership, this strategy appealed to a younger generation, and together they formed the Christian Community Development Association.

My time with John confirmed what I had known for some time, namely, that discipleship in America had to become urban in its vision of usefulness. America was now an urban society. Without realizing it, I had been teaching this since I came to Fuller. Whether the course was evangelism or preaching, the context of effective leadership was urban.

It was not an easy sell among students, and it was not on the agenda among faculty colleagues in the school of world mission. For me, this was strange because it is clear from the New Testament that the early church was conceived in an urban world. From Jerusalem to the uttermost parts was the command. And those parts led ultimately to Rome. But they also passed through much of Asia Minor. We studied Paul's journeys but failed to note that they were centered in the cities of the Middle East. From Damascus to Rome. It is estimated that in his lifetime the apostle Paul traveled more than ten thousand miles in the service of the gospel. The churches that were founded were for the most part in urban centers. My teachers who urged us to go into all the world failed to tell us that even in the New Testament that world was an urban world.

By the time I came to Fuller in 1974, I had become a writer. *My Friend, the Enemy* had been a success and in a way helped legitimate my becoming a member of the faculty. Fuller's faculty was expected to write.

But my writing did not begin with *My Friend, the Enemy* in 1968. There had been a time when I realized that I liked to write. That didn't mean that I was a writer, but I came to know that there was power in words committed to paper.

It began with my work at Cedine Bible Camp in Tennessee. My roommate at Fort Wayne Bible College had signed on there, and I spent several summers on the team working with young people. I was camp director for one year. I came to appreciate what was being done there more so than at camps in the North. Black young people from southern locales brought a different curiosity to the setting, a different eagerness to learn that pulled on all of us. This was a special place.

I had formed friendships with talented young adults in the Detroit network of Assemblies. They accompanied me on several occasions to the summer site. One of them, a gifted young woman, had a fine Pontiac sports sedan, and together with several others we motored from Detroit to Spring City. Traveling by car was fun, and it gave us a chance to thumb our noses at southern racism that would refuse to serve us in restaurants. We packed our own rations and beverages.

But upon our return to Detroit, we met to discuss how to stay in touch with these young people after summer sessions, during the winter months, and came up with the idea of a magazine-type journal. We would write articles we deemed important to the spiritual lives of the kids, and then run off a number of copies mimeograph-style and mail them to the office in Cedine. They would then run off copies and mail them out to local cities. The system was well received by the leadership.

But I got in trouble with something I wrote. Paul Zimmerman, who had founded Cedine and was its head, was not happy with it. I forget what I had written, but I suspect that it was too political for him, and he surely didn't want the kids to be corrupted by such ideas.

We're talking about the early fifties, which saw the beginnings of the civil rights movement, a movement that was deeply Christian and southern. These kids were Christian and southern and black. But the leadership of the camp was white, and their support monies came largely from white, conservative churches in the North. I was insensitive to this situation, but it was the beginning of an awareness of the power of words to make an impression among a Christian public.

White leadership understood their presence in Tennessee as that of missionaries. Zimmerman had been disappointed that he could not fulfill his desire to be a missionary in Africa. He had found his mission field in Tennessee, and he did not intend for any Yankees from the North to mess with it. He need not have worried too much. Years later, Tom Skinner and I were invited back for a series with more adult young people. It didn't go well.

Over the years I would meet white people in black settings who felt called to work among "colored people." Often, they were frustrated by their inability to serve the Lord overseas. They showed up in our communities or at our varied ministries wanting to exercise leadership among ministries already established. When we invited them to serve in the kitchen, they disappeared. None of them could bring themselves to respect the cultural challenges posed by black Americans, and they hardly ever adjusted to the movement toward justice as represented by the civil rights movement.

My real experience in writing came at the invitation of Fred Alexander, whom I had met in Cleveland. He was committed to a ministry in the black community and served as a member of a small Bible school, the Baptist Bible Institute. I met him when I accompanied B. M. Nottage, who was to deliver a commencement address at the school.

This was a typical Nottage gesture. The school could hardly afford our gas money from Detroit, but it was part of a black community, and it was the ongoing passion of Nottage to be useful wherever people were trying to serve our people. So, he preached, and I sang a solo.

Afterward, Fred approached me about writing an article for his fledgling journal *Freedom Now*. I became a regular and saw that journal become important among evangelical constituents who wanted something on the cutting edge of urban mission.

The journal was a radical departure for Fred. He belonged to a denomination better known for its ultraconservatism in matters of ecclesial and theological matters.

Fred experienced what most newcomers experienced who moved into urban communities in an attempt to be useful. They discovered that they needed the city more than the city needed them. Those who remained to be useful did so because they allowed the city to convert them. This was becoming true of so-called foreign missions as well.

In a conversation with a leader of one of the country's leading mission agencies, I learned that his group had ceased to recruit at a well-known Bible institute because their students did not have the flexibility to adjust to an urban world. This was one of the key reasons for white flight from urban centers. The white believers took their churches with them because it was one thing to be converted to Jesus but quite another thing to be converted to the city. And their reading of the Scriptures did not include an observation that the New Testament is an urban text. We didn't learn that in Bible school either.

Years later Fred turned the journal over to his son John, a talented scholar, who eventually became a member of the Wheaton College faculty. John changed the name of the journal to *The Other Side*, a change reflective of his broader social concerns. He was becoming a leader among a new generation of Christians who would be dubbed Radical Evangelicals. Those concerns included issues such as AIDS, and the broader question of gay young men and the church. Racism, segregation among the people of God, and the aftermath of wars in Africa and Asia occupied the pages of the journal. And when focused domestically, these issues were urban issues.

The evangelical movement was unprepared to deal with the realities of an urban world. Even a Billy Graham crusade, although held in cities, was inadequate to speak to these realties. Getting saved, in the language of the times, was important, and there was very little recognition that people in poverty needed more than Jesus. But then poor people did not attend city-wide evangelistic crusades. They couldn't afford the bus fare to the stadium.

24

The Mission Beyond the Mission

In 1983 President Hubbard had decided that the seminary needed to make a statement about the challenges the church and its training institutions faced with a society seemingly losing its moral and ethical core. He drafted what became the seminary's "Mission Beyond the Mission" document. The document was not about methodologies of mission practice but about ethics and the moral demands of the word of God. It was well received across the evangelical network and further cemented Fuller as a leader in the movement.

The document came into being because the seminary had become three schools: theology, world mission and institute of church growth, and psychology. Its intent was not to recast the identity of the school but to affirm the seminary's commitment to discipleship. As the document put it, "We are disciples before we are Christian educators." It was a call to obedience as Christ's disciples to discern the will of God in the world and in the church and to practice his will as Christ's servants.

This would seem to be self-evident for a Christian educational center, but Hubbard, the faculty, and the trustees intended the seminary's publics to know of its broader understanding of discipleship, beyond mere education. The statement centered on five imperatives: go and make disciples, call the church of Christ to renewal, work for the moral health of society, seek peace and justice in the world, and uphold the truth of God's revelation.

Without much previous thought, I found myself responding to the statement. I was proud to support it and had been practicing its basic principles all along. As had our faculty. But the time had come for the seminary to put this in plain sight for students and the broader society.

It was well received among Christian institutions and most evangelicals across the country, and internationally as well. But one issue, that of God's revelation, would come under severe fire in the months ahead as the famous, or infamous, battle for the Bible emerged among evangelicals. One of the more dramatic opportunities to practice the statement's call to make disciples came about when I met the General Secretary of the World Council of Churches (WCC). Dr. Emilio Castro was the dinner guest of Doris and Peter Wagner, and they invited Hazel and me to join them. Castro was from Uruguay, with his office in Geneva, Switzerland. It was a strange gathering. And I have wondered all these years why Peter set it up. He had something in mind besides dinner. I knew that Castro and Wagner could not agree theologically on the church's call to evangelize the world. Wagner, and in fact the majority of the faculty in the school of world mission, understood evangelism as separate from the broader call to engage the political issues associated with injustice in society. Indeed, Wagner hesitated to join the mission faculty until he was convinced that it had not been contaminated by "the liberalism of the school of theology." Liberalism, according to Wagner, was any theology tainted by an association with social justice. Wagner was a mission leader in South America, and it was during the '60s that he was asked to join the SWM faculty. Donald McGavran and Charles Kraft he could respect as disciples of Jesus, but he could not give M. L. King Jr. the same consideration.

He should have known better. McGavran had a liberal streak at the center of his Christian life. He had been a devoted supporter and champion of liberal causes.

The WCC under Castro argued that evangelism and matters of justice were of the same proclamation, part of the call to discipleship. Evangelicals believed in justice but refused to give it equal respect as part of the gospel call to discipleship. I found myself in the middle of that debate. Dinner was delightful, and the Wagners were gracious hosts.

Several months later I was invited to join a conference on evangelism in Geneva. The invitation came from the office of Dr. Castro and would be the first of several visits to that lovely city at the invitation of the WCC. The discussions were lively, and it was clear that within the council there were different convictions regarding the plight of the unreached and the relationship between proclamation and the church's call to justice. I was attracted to the work and witness of a Roman Catholic nun whose parish was in the Philippines. She was passionate about the gospel and the need for its proclamation. I was learning to listen for the voice of the Spirit wherever God's people gathered. Even if they had different nicknames.

Wagner and I became friends—sort of. I thought he had gone off his rocker when he embraced signs and wonders. But he had told me on one occasion that I really belonged in the school of world mission. He knew that I represented evangelism and what little emphasis on missions there was in the school of theology. He was right. In fact, the thought had occurred to me. It could get lonely at times. My colleagues knew that I taught evangelism, and they seemed pleased that I was capable. But I felt that my field did not share the same status as other disciplines associated with theology. After all, Fuller was a theological school. One day Peter took me aside and, looking me in the eye, said, "Bill, you have written the most important book ever written by a member of the theology faculty. But you didn't give us any answers." I was stunned more than flattered by his assertion. I thought that the brother was nuts, but before I could lodge an adequate rejoinder, he told me that an answer had been found.

Afterword

The Gospel According to Bill Pannell

JEMAR TISBY

THE LIGHT SLANTS THROUGH stained glass in long, patient beams, washing the sanctuary in gold and rose. The church carries its age with grace. It's been recently renovated by the new congregation that took up residence there. But they respectfully preserved the bones of the building—arched ceilings, dark wooden pews, a pulpit centered on a raised dais. An homage to the saints who sang, prayed, and preached there long before. But today the air hums with a different kind of presence: the gathered grief and gratitude of people who loved Bill Pannell.

The sanctuary is full. Students, pastors, theologians, and old friends lean close in the pews. Their faces are marked by both respect and wonder, as if we are all trying to comprehend that a man whose words shaped so many of us is no longer here to speak them himself. The sound of the piano rolls softly beneath the murmurs, rising and falling like a tide. The space feels both ancient and alive, which seems fitting. Bill was like that: timeless and timely, rooted and restless, always pressing forward.

I arrive late, as always, and sit near the middle, a program with Bill's face on it delicately cradled in my hand. I already know this is not only a keepsake; as a historian, I view it as an artifact. I'm here as a mourner, not a scholar. Still, as I listen to the low rumble of conversation, fragments of his voice play in my mind—the gravelly warmth, the slow cadence that gave each sentence weight. I think about how often he said things that no one else in the room dared to say, and how he managed to do it without arrogance or apology. "The term ['social action'] is as redundant as 'social gospel,'" he once wrote. "What other kind of gospel is there?"[1]

The service begins. A hush settles, broken only by the rustle of programs. Sunlight shifts across the floor. Someone begins to sing, a hymn older than most of us, and I feel the familiar ache of loss tighten in my chest. I scan the faces—Black, white, Latino, Asian, young and old—and realize that this is one of the few rooms in America where the full breadth of Bill's impact can be seen at once. His influence was never confined to one camp or color. He had the gift of speaking truth in ways that both comforted and convicted, especially those of us who had grown weary of pretending that Christianity and justice were separate callings.

In moments like this, the line between memory and prophecy blurs. It's hard not to imagine Bill sitting in one of these pews, arms crossed, eyes narrowed, a knowing smile creeping up as he surveys the crowd. He would have had something witty to say about the fact that people who once tiptoed around his critiques now quote him like Scripture. He would have told us not to make him into a saint—saints are too easy to ignore.

When I first met Bill, I was a young scholar still in the process of earning my PhD in history. I wanted to research the history of Black evangelicals. I was looking into the evangelist Tom Skinner, and Pannell's name kept coming up. On a whim, I did an internet search and was delighted to find he was still in Fuller Seminary's orbit. To my further surprise, when I emailed him, he replied and agreed to have a phone conversation with me. That began a decade-long correspondence that led to many conversations in his home in Pasadena and a mentorship I cherish to this day. He had a way of saying things so plainly that you couldn't dodge them. It wasn't performative provocation as so many voices are today. It was moral clarity.

As I look around this refurbished sanctuary—this place where the old and new found a way to coexist—I think of how much that mirrors the work Bill did his entire life. He refused to throw away the church, even when it wounded him. He believed that faith was worth redeeming, that institutions could be reformed, and that people could change, though never without discomfort. "Somehow in my lifetime," he once reflected, "the evangelical movement became more and more American and less and less

1. William E. Pannell, *The Coming Race Wars: A Cry for Justice, from Civil Rights to Black Lives Matter*, exp. ed. (Downers Grove, IL: InterVarsity, 2021), 162. The first edition of this book was published in 1993.

Christian. They lost their prophetic edge." That prophetic edge is what we've come to remember today. But it's also what we'll need for the days ahead.

Because as I sit in this sun-drenched sanctuary in Pasadena, I can't help but think about the social and political storms still raging outside these walls. Bill's death in 2024 comes at a time when the nation feels irreconcilably divided. When the line between racism, religion, and politics blurs into the dangerous fusion we call white Christian nationalism. When the same forces he warned us about have grown bolder and more organized. In such vexing times, I feel the weight of his absence. My mind reaches instinctively for his voice, for the way he could slice through confusion with one sharp sentence. I find myself thinking, I wish I could talk to Bill.

When Prophets Seem Scarce

When prophets die, the air feels thinner. The noise of the world rushes in to fill the space they once occupied. As the tributes begin—stories of mentorship, laughter, small rebellions told with affection—I realize how much of Bill's ministry was about disruption for the sake of clarity. He refused to let anyone confuse politeness with holiness. "Don't preach love to me," he once wrote, "especially if you intend that I do all the loving."

It's hard not to think of how that line still lands in our current moment. I hear the echo of it every time someone insists that calls for justice are "too divisive," every time a church prays for unity while systemic and historic wounds remain untreated. Bill knew the danger of a Christianity that prizes civility over conviction. He had lived through it—in the segregated pews, in the polite racism of missions boards, in the quiet exclusions that came disguised as "doctrinal concerns."

The mid-2010s, where his manuscript left off, now seem almost desirable compared to where we stand today. The past decade has tested the moral fiber of US Christianity in ways few of us could have predicted. I think back to Ferguson in 2014—the haunting image of protestors with their hands raised, facing police in riot gear. The chant, "No justice, no peace," rising like a psalm of lament. That was the same year the nation learned the names of Michael Brown, Eric Garner, and Tamir Rice. The same year the phrase Black Lives Matter began to pierce the national conscience.

Bill was already in his eighties then, but he understood what was happening. When we talked, he didn't sound surprised. "America is still a 'pigmentocracy' at its core," he had written years before.[2] For him, the deaths of unarmed Black people were not anomalies—they were symptoms of a spiritual disease that had yet to be healed.

The following years would bring no shortage of evidence. Philando Castile's blood on a Minnesota street. The Mother Emanuel massacre in Charleston, where worshipers were murdered during a Bible study meeting. The Charlottesville rally where torches lit up the night and a crowd chanted, "You will not replace us."[3]

I imagine Bill watching those scenes unfold on the evening news, his jaw tightening, his eyes narrowing not in disbelief but in recognition. He'd been warning the church about this for decades—that a faith intertwined with whiteness would eventually produce this kind of fruit. "The root determines the fruit," as the saying goes.

And then came the election of 2016. I remember watching the results late into the night in bewilderment and silence. Moments like those are when Bill's voice is most needed. If I had spoken to him that night, I'm sure he would have seen it clearly—how fear had fused with faith, how nostalgia masqueraded as theology, how white grievance had been baptized as gospel.

For all the headlines and hashtags, what struck me most about those years was how familiar it all felt. Bill had already mapped this terrain—what happens when the church mistakes empire for kingdom, when it trades its prophetic edge for political access. "White Americans wanted a leader for white America," he wrote about the Reagan era, but the line could have been penned yesterday.[4]

As the decade turned, the patterns deepened. Politicians wrapped the flag around the cross until the two were indistinguishable. The language of "religious freedom" became a weapon to preserve privilege. Church members exited their faith communities over whether saying Black Lives Matter was an act of faith or heresy.[5]

Bill would not have been shocked by the resurgence of white Christian nationalism, though he would have grieved it. He understood that

2. Pannell, *Coming Race Wars*, 92.

3. David Neiwert, "When White Nationalists Chant Their Weird Slogans, What Do They Mean?" SPLC, October 10, 2017, https://www.splcenter.org/resources/hatewatch/when-white-nationalists-chant-their-weird-slogans-what-do-they-mean/.

4. Pannell, *Coming Race Wars*, 63.

5. Campbell Robertson, "A Quiet Exodus," *New York Times*, March 9, 2018, https://www.nytimes.com/2018/03/09/us/blacks-evangelical-churches.html.

whenever the church clings too tightly to power, it loses sight of love. He reminded us that the gospel does not need the government to validate it, and that any faith that demands supremacy has already betrayed its Savior.

As I sit in this memorial service, listening to colleagues recount his teaching years at Fuller Seminary, I think about what kind of courage it took for him to stay there—to carve out space for Black thought and witness in a largely white institution, to insist that his presence was not a gift from them but a grace from God. That, too, was a kind of prophecy: not the mystical prediction of future events, but the quiet, stubborn insistence on telling inconvenient truths in the present. He wrote, "Whatever spirituality is—and there is no one definition to satisfy us all—it is more than a personal experience. If it is the life of God within, it ought to address the way we live our lives publicly."[6] That was Bill's understanding of the gospel—a prophetic, loving, Christ-centered way of being.

The service moves on, but my thoughts drift again to the present: to the current Speaker of the House quoting Scripture to justify exclusion, to state officials buying "Trump Bibles" for classrooms, to entire political movements that use the name of Jesus as a weapon against the vulnerable.[7] I can almost hear Bill's dry chuckle. He'd have called it what it is: idolatry dressed up in patriotism.

And that is why, as the memorial continues, my grief mingles with gratitude. Because even in death, Bill Pannell gives us language for the times we're in. He trained us not to panic when prophets seem scarce, but to remember that prophecy itself never dies—it just waits for new voices willing to speak.

The Gospel According to Bill Pannell

I'll forever be grateful for whatever conversation led to the creation of a documentary about Bill while he was still alive. *The Gospel According to Bill Pannell* is the most accessible distillation of his life and thought. From there, of course, one should go deeper. Read his books. Listen to his sermons. But to hear his voice, trace his long and fruitful life, and listen to the people who knew him best is an experience of Bill that we haven't had

6. Pannell, *Coming Race Wars*, 161.

7. Jill Colvin, "Trump Is Selling 'God Bless the USA' Bibles for $59.99 as He Faces Mounting Legal Bills," *Associated Press*, March 26, 2024, https://apnews.com/article/trump-god-bless-usa-bible-greenwood-2713fda3efdfa297d0f024efb1ca3003.

before. The documentary is both an homage to a faithful Christian man and an inheritance of wisdom passed down to future generations.

Bill spent decades translating the good news into a language that refused to separate salvation from liberation, or faith from justice. His gospel was deeply personal, but never private. In the past decade, the church in America has wrestled with a crisis of identity. White Christian nationalism, once whispered in backrooms and pews, has gone mainstream. Its adherents claim to defend faith, but their faith has become indistinguishable from political ideology. They wave crosses and flags in the same breath, baptizing fear as theology and resentment as righteousness.

I think of Project 2025, the sprawling policy blueprint for a "Christian nation," promising to reshape government in the image of a narrow faith. Its authors talk of "restoring Judeo-Christian tradition," but what they mean is returning power to those who already have it.[8] Bill would have recognized this immediately as a counterfeit gospel—a political religion that uses Jesus as a mascot for domination.

I think of white Christian nationalism—an ethnocultural ideology that uses Christianity as a permission structure for the acquisition of political power and social control. It has shown up in increasingly public ways. There was the January 6 insurrection where a huge wooden cross, Scripture verses emblazoned on signs, and Bibles toted in backpacks went hand in hand with violence and destruction.[9] There were the more quotidian examples: the US flag standing alongside pulpits in churches, celebrations of the Fourth of July as if it was a liturgical holiday, the assumption that one political party was the true "Christian" party.

That's the difference between the gospel according to Bill Pannell and the gospel according to white Christian nationalism. One is a vision of a kingdom without walls. The other is a bunker masquerading as a church. Bill's gospel was rooted in what Jesus announced in Nazareth: good news for the poor, freedom for the captives, sight for the blind (Luke 4:16–19). It was global, not tribal; liberating, not nostalgic; truthful, even when truth cut across political loyalties. "What right does the oppressor have," Bill

8. Paul Dans and Steven Groves, eds., *Mandate for Leadership: The Conservative Promise, Project 2025 Presidential Transition Project* (Washington, DC: Heritage Foundation, 2023), 581.

9. Amanda Tyler, ed., *Christian Nationalism and the January 6 Insurrection*, Baptist Joint Committee for Religious Liberty and the Freedom from Religion Foundation, February 9, 2022, https://bjconline.org/wp-content/uploads/2022/02/Christian_Nationalism_and_the_Jan6_Insurrection-2-9-22.pdf.

asked, "to demand that his victim be saved from sin? You may be scripturally and evangelistically correct, but you're ethically wrong."[10] His gospel could not be co-opted by empire because it was born from the underside of it. It spoke with the authority of those who had endured exclusion and found that the love of Christ was stronger than the gates that kept them out.

The difference between Bill's gospel and the one preached by white Christian nationalists is not merely political—it's theological. One begins with the incarnation, God entering human suffering. The other begins with self-preservation, God securing human comfort. One calls us to humility and repentance. The other baptizes arrogance and power. The gospel according to Bill Pannell was never about safety. It was about solidarity. It was about following Jesus into the hard places, where truth and love often make enemies. He believed that the cross was not just a symbol of salvation but a critique of empire. To believe in the resurrection, Bill reminded us, is to believe that no injustice is final. And so, he kept teaching, kept writing, kept showing up to mentor younger generations—even when his own body began to fail.

At Fuller Seminary, where he taught for four decades, Bill's presence was itself a kind of counter-liturgy. He embodied what it meant to belong to an institution without being owned by it. His office became a sanctuary for students who felt unseen, unheard, or uninvited into the theological conversation. His mentorship was not sentimental. It was demanding. He expected honesty, courage, and humor in equal measure.

As the years went on, and the nation's fractures deepened, I began to understand more clearly what he had been doing all along. Bill wasn't merely critiquing the church; he was rebuilding it from within—one student, one sermon, one act of integrity at a time.

That's the part of his gospel we most need now—liberation. Because white Christian nationalism thrives on fear: fear of losing control, fear of diversity, fear of truth. Bill's gospel was rooted in liberation. The freedom that comes from knowing you are loved without condition. The freedom to tell the truth, even when it costs you something. The freedom to build institutions that outlast the headlines. When the world tempts us to confuse faith with fear, Bill's life reminds us that the gospel does not need our protection—it needs our participation.

In the sanctuary at Bill's memorial, my eyes keep drifting to the picture on the front of the program. It's a picture of Bill wearing a black sweater on

10. William E. Pannell, *My Friend, the Enemy* (Waco, TX: Word, 1968), 64.

a dark background. Only his face stands out. His eyes seem lit from within, a spark from the Holy Spirit that had long ago taken up residence in his heart. He seems to be staring directly at me. He's smiling. It's an encouraging look. As if to say, "Keep preaching the gospel."

A Pandemic and a Protest

It begins, as so many turning points do, with silence.

The streets go quiet in the spring of 2020. The air feels heavy, as if the world itself is holding its breath. Churches shutter their doors. Sanctuaries that once echoed with hymns and sermons now sit hollow, their pews covered in dust and disinfectant. We worship through screens, our faces reflected back at us like icons of isolation.

During the pandemic years, I found myself returning to his books more often. The isolation of COVID-19 revealed how fragile our communities really were. Churches fought over masks, vaccines, and mandates, while neglecting the deeper question: what does love of neighbor look like when the air your neighbor exhales could harm you? The gospel according to Bill Pannell could have helped us. Understanding that the Christian faith was about more than personal liberty to do whatever we desired. It was about the freedom to love others as ourselves, and to pursue their highest good. Bill insisted that caring for the vulnerable was as much a public testimony as any sermon.

Then came the summer of 2020. George Floyd's murder on a Minneapolis street, caught on camera for the world to see. The video of George Floyd's final moments spreads faster than the virus ever could. A knee on a neck, eight minutes and forty-six seconds. The sound of him calling for his mother. The rawness of it cuts through every illusion of progress. There was Breonna Taylor, gunned down in her own home in a disastrous raid by police. We also learned of Ahmaud Arbery, chased down by vigilantes on a Georgia road. The grief was suffocating, the protests relentless, the calls for justice unmistakably moral.

Bill was not surprised by the cruelty of it all. He wrote, "The truth is that the history of America is one unending war against people of color."[11] But he never lost the note of hope and defiance. He always believed that the Spirit of God shows up most clearly among those who cry out for justice. In the rhythmic call and response of protest, I hear something ancient. It

11. Pannell, *Coming Race Wars*, 167.

sounds like the psalms—lament and hope in the same breath. It sounds like the prophets—Amos thundering, "Let justice roll down like waters." The streets had become sanctuaries, the chants a kind of liturgy.

The church, meanwhile, seemed to fracture under the weight of the moment. Some rediscovered the prophetic edge Bill had long urged them to reclaim. Others retreated into silence or backlash. The same pastors who had quoted Martin Luther King Jr. every January now warned their congregations that "social justice" was a distraction from the gospel. Bill had heard that refrain for sixty years. His response was simple: There is no gospel without justice.

"Faith," he once said, "must be lived among the people, not apart from them. Otherwise it becomes a museum exhibit—revered but irrelevant." I imagine how frustrated he would have felt watching the church argue about the inconveniences of masks while morgues filled beyond capacity. For Bill, the crisis of the pandemic would have been a theological one. How we treated one another in our fear, our loneliness, our fatigue—this was a test of what we actually believed about love.

Bill always insisted that the gospel had to touch the ground. It wasn't enough to affirm creeds; you had to embody compassion. He would have seen these marches as sacred spaces—sanctuaries in motion, where the Spirit moved among those who dared to believe that another world was possible.

The summer of 2020 was also a season of exposure. It revealed not only the wounds of society but the fractures within the church. Some Christians joined the movement for justice; others denounced it as Marxist or divisive. Pulpits that had long avoided politics suddenly became battlegrounds. Congregations split over whether to say "Black Lives Matter" or whether those words were too worldly for Sunday mornings.

Bill would have recognized the irony. He had spent his life urging the church to confront racism precisely because of the gospel, not in spite of it. "Reconciliation," he wrote, "is a biblical word. It is *our* word, and its ministry is *our* enterprise. . . . Truly that should be at the core of our curriculum."[12] But reconciliation, for Bill, was never sentimental. It wasn't the handshake at the end of a diversity workshop. It was the costly, daily work of truth-telling and repair. You can't reconcile what you refuse to name. He believed in the kind of peace that came only after confession, not avoidance.

12. Pannell, *Coming Race Wars*, 155.

As the months progressed, as statues fell and slogans filled the air, I found myself returning to his words again and again. He had taught me that every generation faces its own test of courage. For his, it was desegregation and the long struggle for civil rights. For ours, it is resisting the ways Christian nationalism seeks to baptize cruelty. The question, he might say, is not whether we will be political, but whether we will be faithful. The pandemic and the protests intertwined—one exposed the frailty of our bodies, the other the sickness of our souls. Together, they formed a mirror.

By 2021, the world had changed again. Vaccines rolled out, churches reopened, and yet the divisions deepened. School boards debated whether children should learn about slavery or systemic racism. Politicians claimed that teaching history honestly was itself an act of hate. The backlash came swift and loud, clothed in religious language. Through it all, I often looked to Bill, either in his books or in our conversations.

So many other leaders, even Black people, were interested in keeping the peace, not making it. I had seen plenty of well-meaning folks become overly accommodationist to ongoing racial harm and white cultural sensibilities. They would tiptoe around the honest truth that needed to be shared with the powers that be. Not Bill. I remember sitting in his living room for hours talking about the events of the day. In all his analysis, he remained Black-centered. He never soft-pedaled the truth about racism. He never resorted to bothsidesism. He never made false equivalencies or blamed Black people for our continued struggles in this country. He always recognized racism as a problem coming from "my friend the enemy." Somehow he was able to hold this clear-eyed assessment and yet remain in vital relationships with some of them.

Maybe his boldness made some people uncomfortable, but it was the discomfort that comes with telling the truth rather than simply giving people what their itching ears wanted to hear. He was never interested in easy victories. He wanted integrity, even if it cost you comfort. And so, while some pastors tried to keep everyone happy, Bill would have urged them to tell the truth—about race, about history, about the complicity of the church. Because silence, he knew, is never neutral.

When I look back now, it seems the world we inhabit is one Bill tried to prepare us for. The same structures of power he critiqued in the twentieth century have simply changed their slogans for the twenty-first. The same evasions of conscience, the same fear of losing control, the same tendency to confuse nationalism for holiness.

But there's something else he prepared us for too: endurance. He had a stubborn faith that God's story was bigger than any empire's. He believed that hope, rightly understood, is not optimism—it's obedience. It's the discipline of believing that justice will have the final word, even when the evidence says otherwise.

As I sit in this Pasadena sanctuary, I can almost feel that endurance rising from the walls. The people here—students, pastors, neighbors—carry the quiet conviction that the story isn't over. Bill may be gone, but his gospel still breathes. When the choir begins to sing "Great Is Thy Faithfulness," the sound fills every corner. The pandemic, the protests, the polarization—they all seem to hang in the air, waiting for interpretation. And in the echo of that hymn, I find it. Bill's life was the interpretation. He spent nine and a half decades showing us that faithfulness is not nostalgia for the past; it's the courage to love the world as it is and still believe it can be made new.

Building What Endures

There's a rhythm to every memorial service: grief, laughter, resolve. We tell stories to soften the loss and remind ourselves that a life like Bill's cannot be buried. When the formal program ends, people linger in the aisles. Old students reunite with professors, pastors trade stories about sermons that shaped them, and a few stand quietly near the front, lost in thought.

That's when it hits me—not the sadness of his absence but the sheer scope of what he left behind. Bill was never content to simply critique institutions. He built them. In a world where so many prophetic voices burn out or get pushed out, he somehow found a way to carve out space and stay. That, to me, remains one of his greatest miracles.

I often tell people that when you work for racial justice in historically white institutions, one of three things happens: you sell out, you burn out, or you get pushed out. But Bill chose to transform the space from within without letting it dilute his witness for justice. His chosen ground for that transformation was Fuller Seminary. For forty years, he poured himself into that community—not as an apologist for its shortcomings but as a witness to what it could become. He taught homiletics and evangelism, but what he really taught was courage. He reminded his students that the gospel was not a performance to be perfected but a truth to be lived.

The seminary honored him in 2015 by naming the William E. Pannell Center for Black Church Studies in his honor. This was not simply an academic department. It was an outpost for the Black evangelical witness, for the gospel according to Bill Pannell. It would be a rest stop and haven for Black Christians weary with the racism of the world. It would become a site of learning so others could stand in solidarity with Black people in the struggle for human dignity. In naming the center after him, Fuller Seminary signaled that the Black church tradition was not a footnote to American Christianity but one of its most vital expressions.

Through the Pannell Center, Bill's influence continues to ripple outward. Each lecture, each class, each gathering of students wrestling with faith and justice is a living footnote to his work. "What we should be striving for," Bill wrote, "is a spirituality that will inform both evangelism and social transformation."[13]

That line might as well be the mission statement for the center—and for all of us who continue his work. But Bill's legacy wasn't confined to Fuller. It lived in the countless lives he mentored and the words he left behind. He understood that the written word was itself a form of institution-building. As a historian, one of my guiding principles is that Black people must leave a paper trail. The archives must be filled with our writings, art, newspaper clippings, activism, and theology. We must preserve these for our posterity so they can learn from the Black Christian witness of their forebears. We cannot let others narrate our faith for us. We must record what we have seen and heard of God's work in our midst.

Bill did that, and more. His books—*My Friend, the Enemy*; *Evangelism from the Bottom Up*; *The Coming Race Wars*; this memoir—along with so many essays and sermons, form a spiritual archive of twentieth- and twenty-first-century Black evangelical thought. They are testimonies to both suffering and joy, to the persistent belief that the Spirit still moves in unlikely places. That paper trail is an act of resistance. In a nation that so often tries to erase or rewrite Black faith, every written word becomes a memorial stone. It says: We were here. We believed. We built.

Now, in 2025, those of us who remain are stewards of that record. We're living in a time when institutions—academic, journalistic, even ecclesial—are under attack from leaders who see truth as an obstacle to power. Project 2025's proposed elimination of the Department of Education, for instance, reveals what Bill warned about all along: when ideology replaces theology, learning becomes a threat.[14]

13. Pannell, *Coming Race Wars*, 160.

14. Dans and Groves, eds., *Mandate for Leadership*, 319.

Yet Bill's life stands as a counter-testimony. While others talk of tearing down, he modeled how to build. Not edifices of brick and bureaucracy but communities of trust and accountability. He understood that institutions, for all their flaws, can be vessels of grace when filled with truth. Even now, I can picture him walking through Fuller's campus in the late afternoon, stopping to greet students by name, the California sun reflecting off his glasses. He loved to ask people what they were working on, and he really listened to the answers. That was part of his genius: he made you believe your ideas mattered because, to him, they did.

He once told me that building a legacy isn't about scale—it's about faithfulness. It's about doing what God gives you to do and then getting out of the way. He did that so humbly and effectively. The evidence surrounded me in the sanctuary on the day of his memorial. The builders he spoke of are sitting here today—the students, the preachers, the scholars, the activists, all of us trying to live into the gospel according to Bill Pannell.

In the days leading up to this memorial, I kept thinking about a distinctly Bill Pannell benediction. It was a line from one of his friends: "Love the Lord your God with all your heart, soul, mind, and strength. Then go play." That, I think, is the secret to his endurance. He loved God deeply, worked tirelessly, and still made space for joy. In a world of endless crises, he kept his sense of humor. He knew that laughter, too, is a form of resistance—that joy is proof we have not been conquered.

When I walk out of the sanctuary into the Pasadena sun, I notice the sound of laughter ringing against the old stone walls, echoing across time. It strikes me that this is the truest tribute to Bill Pannell's life: the next generation at play, unafraid, free.

Epilogue: Dreamers' History

The sanctuary is quieter when I go back inside. The crowd has thinned somewhat, and yet no one seems eager to leave. People linger in small circles, trading stories like sacred currency. The hum of conversation sounds like prayer. I linger, too, meeting friends from across Bill's many different but overlapping circles of influence. I let the joy of fellowship wash over me, and I realize that this is not the end of the story. It never was. Bill's passing doesn't close a chapter so much as it turns the page for the rest of us.

In the documentary he said, "History is always in the hands of the dreamers. If you have one . . . tell it." That line has lived in my bones ever since I first heard it. It was more than a call to imagination—it was a summons to responsibility. Because to dream, in Bill's sense, was not escapism. It was defiance. It was the conviction that the future could still be written differently, even when the evidence suggested otherwise.

It's barely been a year since Bill departed this world for the next. And in that time our world has given us plenty of reasons to despair: the rise of authoritarianism, the resurgence of white Christian nationalism, the disintegration of public trust. And yet, standing here in this sanctuary—this space that's both old and reborn—I sense the persistence of his faith.

Bill never confused the church with the kingdom. He knew institutions falter, leaders fail, and movements fracture. But he also believed that God's Spirit outlasts them all. That's why he kept teaching long after retirement age, why he kept writing even when his hands shook, why he kept mentoring when his body grew tired. He believed that faithfulness mattered more than success, that bearing witness was its own kind of victory.

I look again at his photograph and think of all the people who passed through his classroom, his living room, his life. Each one of them carries a piece of his gospel now. It's there in the sermons preached from pulpits across the country, in the justice work of churches that finally found their prophetic edge, in the quiet faith of those who still believe that love can transform the world.

As I leave the sanctuary, sunlight pours through the open doors, flooding the hallway with light. Outside, the city hums—the clatter of traffic, the chatter of pedestrians, the wind in the palm trees. Life, relentless and tender, goes on. For a moment, I think of that refrain that closed the service, the line borrowed from Bill's dear friend Gerry Mann: "Love the Lord your God with all your heart, soul, mind, and strength. Then go play."

That's Bill's gospel in its purest form. Love God. Love people. Don't forget to play. Because joy, he taught us, is not the absence of struggle—it's the evidence of resurrection. So I step into the sunlight, take a deep breath, and imagine his voice one last time—gentle, wry, insistent: "If you've got a dream, tell it."

And I resolve within myself to do just that.

Additional Materials of Interest

Films

Black + Evangelical. Directed by Daniel Long, 2025. https://pages.christianitytoday.com/black-evangelicals-documentary-lp. A documentary from *Christianity Today* and Wheaton College discussing African American Christians within predominantly white evangelicalism. Bill figures prominently.

The Gospel According to Bill Pannell. Directed by Patrick O'Neil Duff, 2024. https://fullerstudio.fuller.edu/feature/the-gospel-according-to-bill-pannell. A documentary from Fuller Seminary and Jemar Tisby using only Bill's voice, archival footage, and interviews with him.

Interviews

William E. Pannell Oral History Interviews. Archives of Wheaton College. https://archives.wheaton.edu/repositories/4/resources/448.

Other Material

Fort Wayne Bible College Light Tower Yearbook, 1951. https://archive.org/details/fortwaynebibleco1951fort. Bill was the yearbook editor and is featured in multiple places. A handwritten inscription from Bill appears on p. 32.

Edward Gilbreath. "My Friend, Bill Pannell." *Christianity Today*, October 14, 2024. https://www.christianitytoday.com/2024/10/my-friend-william-pannell-theologian-reflection/.

Daniel Silliman. "Died: Bill Pannell, Black Evangelical Who Raised the Issue of Racism." *Christianity Today*, October 15, 2024. https://www.christianitytoday.com/2024/10/died-bill-pannell-black-evangelical-white-racism-race-war-friend-enemy/.

"Tom Skinner's 'New Beginning.'" Wheaton Archives and Special Collections, February 1, 2021. https://fromthevault.wheaton.edu/2021/02/01/tom-skinners-new-beginning/. Contains some archival material related to Bill.

Contributors

Anthea Butler is Geraldine R. Segal Emeritus Professor in American Social Thought at the University of Pennsylvania. Professor Butler was the winner of the 2022 Martin Marty Award for the Public Understanding of Religion.

Jemar Tisby is a historian and public intellectual whose work examines race, faith, and US history within the Black Christian tradition. He is the *New York Times* best-selling author of *The Color of Compromise* and *The Spirit of Justice* and serves as research faculty with the Pannell Center for Black Church Studies at Fuller Seminary.

www.ingramcontent.com/pod-product-compliance
Lightning Source LLC
LaVergne TN
LVHW090521110826
845146LV00003B/941

* 9 7 9 8 3 8 5 2 7 7 8 7 2 *